CHOPSTICKS CLEAVER AND WOK

homestyle chinese cooking by Jennie Low

Editor: Doong Tien
Illustrations: Lorrie Farrelly
Cover & Title Page: Susan Bailyn

PREFACE

"CHOPSTICKS, CLEAVER AND WOK" is devoted to assisting you in your pursuit of happiness through creative Chinese cooking. Its objective is to open new doors to the wonderful world of Chinese cuisine.

This book, although arriving late on the current Chinese cookbook scene, has been under way for a number of years. The recipes reveal the artistic and creative ability of Jennie Low, who has drawn upon her many years of experience in daily home cooking and in teaching the art to others.

You will find interesting and informative facts, including both the English and Chinese names for the various dishes, as well as the Chinese characters, English and Chinese names for items included in the "Tea Lunch" and "Food Stuffs Used in Chinese Cooking" sections of this book.

It has been my pleasure to know Jennie Low and to experience her cooking and teaching. In creating this unique Chinese cookbook, she presents a "bird's eye view" of the fascinating world of Chinese culinary greatness that **NOW YOU**, too, can share!

Ellen Hoffnagel
Program Director, University YWCA
Berkeley, California

DEDICATION

This book is dedicated to all my friends and students, past and present, who have been so inspirational in its creation. Their continual requests for a compilation of these recipes in book form, their repeated verification as to the clarity of each recipe, and their continuous support of my "project", have resulted in **CHOPSTICKS, CLEAVER, AND WOK.** To each of them, my "Thanks" and my gratitude!

Also a special "Thanks" to Doong Tien for her work on the manuscript, to Susan Bailyn for the cover design, and to Lorrie Farrelly for her sketches.

To my husband John, whose talents and abilities were of great help, and to our very own Cindy and Denise, who assisted me in my cooking classes, I would like to express my deep and lasting appreciation.

AUTHOR'S NOTE

Each time I began a new class, I saw before me a group of faces which seemed to ask the same question . . "Can I, too, cook Chinese?" I told them this story. Fifteen years ago, I arrived in America from Hong Kong. I spoke little English. Worse yet, I knew not how to cook even one grain of rice! My uncle, with whom I stayed, was himself a master chef. Every week on Wednesday, his day off, he would spend the day cooking marvelous foods for his family. He would say to me, "Watch, now, so that you will know how to cook this yourself some day!" But alas! Being young and carefree, I would pay no heed. We would all sit down, eat and enjoy the food to our heart's content, then wash the dishes. And my uncle would say, "Oh, Jennie! How are you ever going to learn how to cook?"

Then one day, I married....as young girls do! And, my husband was one who liked his Chinese food.. food like his mother used to make! What to do? My uncle, having gone on to the big Chinese kitchen in the sky, was no longer around to show me. I asked my Auntie, "Auntie, how do you cook fish heads like his mother used to prepare them?" And Auntie would answer me, "Ask his mother!" But, of course, no way! So then Auntie would tell me, "Chop the fish, give a sprinkle of this, a sprinkle of that, and you have it."

Well, to make a long story short, I did learn to cook, by just that way! "A sprinkle of this and a sprinkle of that"....And if it was too salty, then the next time, a little less sprinkle of this, a little more sprinkling of that. By this method, I have today more than one hundred recipes. Some of my favorite recipes I am sharing with you! Each recipe has been developed by first cooking the dish in my customary way; then through painstaking measuring, the flavor of each original dish was achieved.

I am confident that you, too, will become an expert at Chinese cooking, by faithfully following these recipes....or perhaps you would like to develop your own "sprinkle" system!

 Jennie Low

CONTENTS

Page

PREFACE

DEDICATION

AUTHOR'S NOTE

GENERAL INFORMATION . . . . 1 - 26
    WOK MEI 1
    COOKING UTENSILS 3
    COOKING METHODS 9
    CUTTING TECHNIQUES 13
    INGREDIENTS USED IN CHINESE COOKING 16
    TABLE OF MEASUREMENTS 26

       RECIPES   CHINESE NAME

APPETIZERS . . . . 27 - 34
    CHINESE DOUGHNUTS . . . . JEEN DUI 27
    CHINESE FRIED DUMPLINGS . . . . JOW GWOK JAI 30
    EGG ROLLS . . . . CHOON GUEN 31
    SHRIMP BALLS . . . . HA KAU 33
    SHRIMP TOAST . . . . HA DOH SEE 34

SOUPS . . . . 35 - 50, 146
    BASIC NOODLE SOUP . . . . TONG MEIN 35
    BIRD'S NEST SOUP . . . . YIN WAU TONG 36
    CHICKEN MEATBALL SOUP . . . . GAI KAU TONG 37
    CHICKEN WHISKY SOUP . . . . GAI JAU TONG 38
    EGG FLOWER SOUP . . . . GAI DON TONG 39
    *HOT AND SOUR SOUP . . . . SHEUN LOT TONG 40
    LETTUCE SOUP . . . . TSANG CHOY TONG 42
    LOTUS ROOT SOUP . . . . LIN NGAU TONG 43

SOUPS (Continued)	CHINESE NAME	Page
RICE SOUP . . . (Congee)	JOOK	44
WITH BEEF	NGOW YUK JOOK	45
WITH CHICKEN	GAI KAU JOOK	45
WITH PORK MEATBALLS	GEE YUK JOOK	46
SEAWEED SOUP	GEE CHOY TONG	47
*SIZZLING RICE SOUP	WOH BAH TONG	48
WATERCRESS SOUP	SAI YONG CHOY TONG	49
WINTER MELON SOUP	DOONG GWAH TONG	50
WON TON SOUP	TONG WON TON	146
POULTRY		51 - 73
BEAN SAUCE CHICKEN	MIN SEE GAI	51
BOILED CHICKEN, CANTONESE	BOK CHEET GAI	52
CASHEW NUT CHICKEN	YIU GWOH GAI	54
CHICKEN WITH ASPARAGUS	LEE SUN GAI KAU	56
CHICKEN WITH BEAN CAKE SAUCE	FOO YUEH GAI	57
CHICKEN WITH CABBAGE	GAI CHOW YEH CHOY	58
CHICKEN SALAD, CANTONESE	SAU SEE GAI	59
COLD CHICKEN WITH ASPARAGUS	DOONG LEE SUN GAI	61
CRISPY CHICKEN	CHUI PEI GAI	62
CURRIED CHICKEN WITH POTATOES	GAH-LI GAI	63
DUCK AND POTATOES	SHEU-JAI MUN OP	64
FRIED CHICKEN, CANTONESE	JOW GAI	66
FRIED SQUAB, CANTONESE	JOW BOK GOP	67
GIZZARDS, CANTONESE	SEE YAU GAI SUN	68
PAPER WRAPPED CHICKEN	GEE-BOW GAI	69
PINEAPPLE CHICKEN	BWO LUO GAI	71
SOY SAUCE CHICKEN WINGS	SEE YAU GAI YICK	72
STEAMED CHICKEN, CANTONESE	JING GAI	73

				Page
EGGS	**CHINESE NAME**			**74 - 78**
EGG FOO YUNG	FOO YUNG DON			74
EGG FOO YUNG GRAVY	FOO YUNG DON HU SIU			75
EGGS WITH GREEN PEAS AND SHRIMP	CHIANG DOW DON			76
STEAMED EGGS, CANTONESE	JING SHUI DON			77
STEAMED EGG CUSTARD	TIEM DON FAH			78
MEAT . . . . BEEF				**79 - 85**
BEEF IN HOISIN SAUCE	HOISIN JERNG NGOW YUK			79
BEEF IN OYSTER SAUCE	HO YAU NGOW YUK			80
BEEF STEW, CANTONESE	NGOW NOM			81
BEEF WITH FUZZY SQUASH	MO GWAH NGOW YUK			82
CURRIED TRIPE	GA-LI NGOW TU			83
GROUND BEEF & NAPA CABBAGE	NGOW YUK SIU CHOY			84
TOMATO BEEF	FON KEHR NGOW YUK			85
MEAT . . . . PORK				**86 - 98**
CHINESE BARBECUED PORK	CHA SIU			86
HAM WITH BEAN THREADS	HUO TUI FUN SEE			87
HOISIN SAUCE SPARERIBS	HOISIN JERNG PAI GWUT			88
PIGS FEET IN VINEGAR SAUCE	SHEUN GEE GURK			89
PORK AND CHINESE SAUSAGE CAKES, STEAMED .	GEE YUK BEHNG			90
PORK SPARERIBS WITH BLACK BEAN SAUCE . . .	SEE JUP PAI GWUT			91
PORK WITH PICKLED MUSTARD	JAH CHOY GEE YUK			93
PORK WITH STRING BEANS	DOW GAWK GEE YUK			94
STEAMED PORK WITH CHINESE RADISH	CHOY PO JING GEE YUK			95
SWEET AND SOUR PORK	TIM-SHEUN YUK			96
TWICE COOKED PORK	HUI WAW YUK			98
SEAFOOD				**99 - 111**
ABALONE IN OYSTER SAUCE	HO YAU BAU YEU			99
ABALONE WITH BOK CHOY	BAU YEU BOK CHOY			100
CASHEW NUT PRAWNS	YIU GWOH HA			101

SEAFOOD (Continued)	CHINESE NAME	Page
CURRIED PRAWNS	GA-LI HA	102
ORIENTAL PAN-FRIED PRAWNS	JEEN HA	103
SHELLING & DEVEINING A PRAWN	HEE HA CHERNG	104
SPICED SHRIMP	LAHT HA	105
STEAMED PRAWNS WITH BLACK BEANS	SEE JUP JING HA	106
STEAMED SALMON, CANTONESE	JING SA-MON YEU	107
STEAMED SAND DAB	JING TOP SAH YEU	108
STIR-FRIED CRAB	CHOW HAI	109
HOW TO PREPARE LIVE CRAB FOR COOKING	JU HAI FONG FAT	110
SQUID WITH SNOW PEAS	CHOW YAU YEU	111

VEGETABLES		113 - 127
BEAN SPROUTS WITH MIXED VEGETABLES	CHOW NGAH CHOY	113
BROCCOLI WITH CHICKEN	GAI CHOW GUY LON	114
CHINESE MUSHROOMS WITH BAMBOO SHOOTS	DOONG GOO JOOK SUN	115
CHINESE STRING BEANS WITH PRAWNS	DOW GOK CHOW HA KAU	116
CHOW BEAN CAKE	CHOW DOW FOO	117
HOT PEPPER TOSS	LAHT JIU SOONG	118
LOTUS ROOT WITH PORK	LIN NGAU CHOW GEE YUK	119
MUSHROOMS IN OYSTER SAUCE	HO YAU DOONG GOO	120
*NORTHERN VEGETABLES COVERED WITH EGG	WAU CHOY DAI MO	121
*SPICED CABBAGE	LOT YEH CHOY	122
*SPICED EGGPLANT	LOT KER JEE	123
SPINACH WITH BEAN CAKE PASTE	FU YEUH BWO CHOY	124
STIR-FRIED BOK CHOY	CHOW BOK CHOY	125
STUFFED BEAN CAKES	YEUNG DOW FOO	126
STUFFED BEAN CAKES, STEAMED	JIN YEUNG DOW FOO	127
STUFFED BEAN CAKES IN BROTH	YEUNG DOW FOO TONG	127

Page

NOODLES . . . . CHINESE NAME . . . . 128 - 136

    BEEF CHOW MEIN . . . . NGOW YUK CHOW MEIN 128

    CHICKEN CHOW MEIN . . . . GAI CHOW MEIN 130

    CHICKEN TOPPING ON NOODLES . . . . GAI KOW MEIN 131

    NOODLES IN GRAVY . . . . YEE MEIN 133

    NOODLES IN OYSTER SAUCE . . . . GON LO MEIN 134

    *SPICED NOODLES . . . . JA JEUNG MEIN 135

    TOMATO BEEF CHOW MEIN . . . . FON KERR NGOW YUK CHOW MEIN 136

RICE . . . . 138 - 140

    FRIED RICE . . . . CHOW FON 138

    STEAMED RICE . . . . BOK FON 139

    SWEET RICE . . . . GNAW MAI FON 140

WON TON . . . . 141 - 146

    BASIC WON TON . . . . WON TON HAUM 141

    HOW TO WRAP WON TON . . . . BAU WON TON 142

    DEEP-FRIED WON TON . . . . JOW WON TON 143

    WON TON IN GRAVY . . . . MUN YEE WON TON 144

    WON TON IN OYSTER SAUCE . . . . HO YAU GON LO WON TON 145

    WON TON SOUP . . . . TONG WON TON 146

MISCELLANEOUS . . . . 147 - 162

    ALMOND MILK CURD . . . . HUNG YUN DOW FOO 147

    BARBECUED PORK BUN . . . . CHA SIU BOW 148

    FRESH COCONUT & PRESERVED SWEET AND

      SOUR GINGER . . . . YEH GEE TIM-SHEUN GERNG 151

    HOT SPICED OIL . . . . LAHT YAU 152

    *MANDARIN GLAZED APPLE & BANANA . . . . . . BUT SEE PING GWO HERNG JIU 153

    *MONGOLIAN FIRE POT . . . . DAH BIEN LOO 154

    NEW YEAR'S CAKE . . . . NIEN GOH 156

    PICKLED CARROTS & DAIKON RADISH . . . . SHEUN LAW BOK 157

MISCELLANEOUS (Continued)   **CHINESE NAME**   **Page**

PICKLED MUSTARD GREENS . . . . SHEUN GUY CHOY 158

*POT STICKERS . . . . HUO TIP 159

STEAMED PORK DUMPLINGS . . . . SHIU MAI 161

SHAPING A PORK DUMPLING . . . . JU SHIU MAI FONG FAT 162

TEA LUNCH INFORMATION . . . . YUM CHA 163

FOOD STUFFS USED IN CHINESE COOKING . . . . . . JOP FUO 168

CHINESE BANQUET INFORMATION . . . . IN WUI 174

SUGGESTED BANQUET MENUS . . . . IN WUI CHOY DON 175

INDEX

*NORTHERN RECIPES   **BEI FONG CHOY**

HOT & SOUR SOUP . . . . SHEUN LOT TONG 40

NORTHERN VEGETABLES COVERED WITH EGG . . WAU CHOY DAI MO 121

SIZZLING RICE SOUP . . . . WOH BAH TONG 48

SPICED CABBAGE . . . . LOT YEH CHOY 122

SPICED EGGPLANT . . . . LOT KER JEE 123

SPICED NOODLES . . . . JA JEUNG MEIN 135

MANDARIN GLAZED APPLE & BANANA . . . . . . BUT SEE PING GWO HERNG JIU 153

MONGOLIAN FIRE POT . . . . DAH BIEN LOO 154

POT STICKERS . . . . HUO TIP 159

WOK MEI

All good Chinese cooks strive for **WOK MEI**. What then, is "wok mei"? **WOK MEI** is the indescribable attribute of good cooking, especially stir-fry. "Ho wok mei" is the ultimate compliment that one can give to the Chinese cook. I would describe **WOK MEI** as being the satisfaction of each of the five senses (sight, smell, taste, texture and temperature) imparted by a well prepared culinary dish.

A food creation contributes **WOK MEI** by being pleasing to the **eye**. For example, sweet and sour foods are basically red in color. But, by adding slices of green pepper, contrast in color is added and contributes to the recipe's "wok mei". The same effect is achieved by the Chinese cook's generous use of coriander (Chinese parsley).

The **aroma** of a dish contributes to **WOK MEI**. It is well known--food that smells good, tastes good. Every dish should impart its own distinctive aroma. Here is the secret for imparting aroma, or "heung" to your Chinese cooking.

Before stir-frying, always heat the wok to a high temperature. It is not hot enough until the wok begins to smoke. Then add the cooking oil, and if called for by the recipe, the garlic and ginger. Allow these to sizzle and burn a little before you add your main ingredients. Temperature control is critical; it must not be too hot or, worse, not hot enough for the food you are preparing. A "feel" for the correct temperature will come with your experience in cooking with the wok.

Taste gives **WOK MEI** to a dish. Each recipe tells you how much salt, how much pepper, etc., I have found to be satisfactory. But, **you** may find my choice of spices too salty, or too peppery for **your** taste. Good "wok mei" then, is partly using the spices so as to be satisfying to **your** liking. And, if you should season your food so as to satisfy most of your guests' taste, then you will have attained one of the necessary components for good "wok mei".

The fourth component of good Wok Mei is **texture**. All foods have their own natural textures. Meat is tender, chewy. Broccoli, celery and carrots have a very crispy texture. Bean curds are firm, yet soft. Spaghetti and noodles are ideally cooked "al dente". The good cook strives to preserve the texture of foods in the cooking process. When cooking vegetables by the stir-fry method, texture is preserved by the strict attention to cooking time and to the temperature of the wok. For instance, celery and broccoli are cooked in just a few short minutes in the wok over high heat. The constant stirring and moving of the contents in the wok allows the cooking without the destruction of the natural texture of foods.

Finally, Wok Mei demands the serving of food at its proper **temperature**. Hot foods should be served **HOT**, cold foods should be served **COLD**. Stir-fried foods should always be served at the table immediately after turning out from the wok.

This is my humble attempt at describing the intangible Wok Mei. Some cooks achieve it naturally with everything they cook, even when simply frying an egg. Other cooks may strive for years, and never achieve it. May you receive many compliments of **"HO WOK MEI"** for every dish you serve!

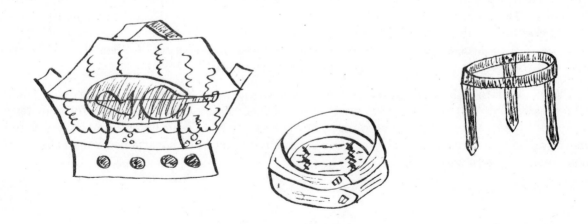

CHOPSTICKS

The Chinese use chopsticks as easily and naturally as forks are used by Europeans.

Oriental chopsticks are extensions of man's fingers. They are remnants of the days when man ate food with his fingers.

There are different kinds of chopsticks. Chinese chopsticks are blunt on the "eating" end. Japanese chopsticks are pointed. There are shorter length chopsticks for children.

Many materials are used in the making of chopsticks. Most common are wood and bamboo. There are also ivory, plastic, silver, and even jade chopsticks. Plastic chopsticks are not very durable, as they eventually warp and bend after repeated cleaning in hot water. For every day use, wooden, bamboo, or ivory chopsticks are best.

Chopsticks are used for cooking as well as eating. After you have become adept in their use, you will find them to be a natural utensil in handling noodles, or in deep-fry cooking. Chinese use them to beat or scramble eggs, and to stir-fry foods in the wok.

All Chinese food is cut and prepared in such a way that it may be handled with chopsticks; therefore, eating with chopsticks should not be too difficult. But, it does require practice! Our fingers have become lazy because we have used forks for so long. Fingers really have to work in order to use chopsticks. So, PRACTICE!

Even rice poses no problem with chopsticks! If you will notice, the Chinese always eats his rice from a bowl. Even he would find it difficult to pick up rice from a plate.

(Plate rice dishes are a Western innovation, and are meant to be eaten Western style, with a fork.) The Chinese eat their rice by putting the rice bowls up to their mouths. The rice is then shoveled into the mouth with the chopsticks. I realize that this method of eating is very foreign to Western etiquette, but when eating rice, do as the Chinese do!!

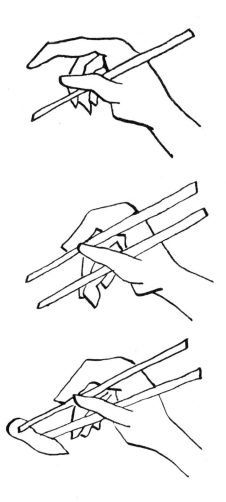

TECHNIQUE IN USING CHOPSTICKS

Eating with chopsticks is not difficult, but it will require some practice! Think of chopsticks as extensions of the fingers, which they are. And, think of them as pincers, which is the principle of their action.

Hold the chopsticks no lower than in the middle. They are ideally held along the upper third of their length. If the sticks are held too low, you will lose much of the "pincer" action.

Practice, first, by picking up large pieces of food, such as chunks of celery or meat. You will have achieved mastery when you can pick up a large button mushroom that is swimming in slippery oyster sauce!

1) Rest one chopstick in the groove of your hand, between the **THUMB** and the **FOREFINGER**. Notice that the **MIDDLE** finger, along with the others, is curved inward to also support the chopstick.

2) With the first chopstick in place, grasp the second stick with the **THUMB** and **FOREFINGER**.

3) Now, operate your chopsticks by first moving the top stick. It is easier to start by first learning to manipulate the stick that is grasped by the thumb and forefinger.

5

THE CLEAVER

To master all the different ways of using the Chinese cleaver would certainly mark one as proficient in the Chinese kitchen. In many restaurants there is often one person who does nothing but cut and chop because of his expertise with the cleaver. His work and its results are truly a joy to behold.

Unlike the French kitchen, where there is a knife for each function, the Chinese cook does all with a single knife, his cleaver. He cuts vegetables, decoratively, finely, or julienne style. He uses it to peel water chestnuts, or apples. An expert fascinates and entertains many children by the simple act of peeling an apple with a cleaver, removing the peel in one long continuous strip! The cleaver is used to mince or to grind meat, in the absence of a modern meat grinder. It is used to chop bones, such as when cutting chicken or spareribs. Because of its broad blade, which acts as a guide, the cleaver slices cheese and lunch meats neatly and evenly.

The blade of the cleaver is used to crush garlic, ginger, or water chestnuts. One good whack with the flat of the blade, or a few quick chops, is all that is necessary to reduce fresh garlic or ginger to proper size.

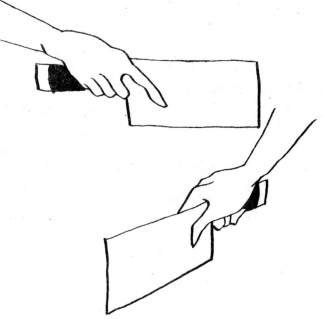

The expert uses even the handle of the cleaver. The butt end is utilized as a pestle to reduce black beans to a paste-like consistency for use. Mastery of the cleaver requires practice. Here are some tips for you to become proficient without losing fingers!

At first glance, the cleaver appears quite formidable as a kitchen utensil. That is good, as it should be handled with care and respect. A little handling will soon acquaint you with its fine balance, and its utility. Cutting large items, such as french bread, watermelon or squash, is a safe and easy way to develop the "feel" of the cleaver. Next, try your hand at slicing ham, cheese, or a roast.

Remember this rule - The cleaver is always used to cut **DOWN** into food, onto a chopping block or cutting board. You will see that the broad, flat blade is an excellent guide for making nice, even slices.

Now as you become more proficient, use your cleaver to cut french fries, celery or carrot sticks. For Chinese cooking, the real skill is to be able to cut these into very thin strips, julienne style. Here is a tip - to avoid cutting the fingers, **CURVE** the fingers when holding, say a carrot. Then the knuckles act as a guide against the blade of the cleaver. Now, as long as you never raise the knife higher than your knuckles, you will never cut yourself. An additional safeguard is to cut downward, slanting the knife slightly **AWAY** from the holding hand.

To **MINCE** meat for Won-Ton filling, or pork cakes, use the cleaver as follows: First, trim the meat of all excess fat. Next, cut the meat into one-inch cubes. Now, chop with the cleaver. Gather and turn the meat often with the cleaver, so as to obtain an even mincing of the meat.

Some cooks prefer to mince meat with two cleavers. Chopping with both hands, they develop a rhythm and a pattern, and finish the job in half the time!

When chopping boney meats with the cleaver, do not place your hand too close to the cut! Practice first with spareribs, where you can hold at the opposite end. Your confidence will develop with experience. Be sure to always chop on a firm surface.

Buying a Cleaver: Cleavers usually come equipped with wooden handles. However, one-piece steel cleavers are available. It is recommended that you purchase the latter if possible. Wooden handles tend to wear and work loose with use, and it becomes a nuisance to continually repair them. Also, cleavers come in different weights. Try to find one that is comfortable for you. The most commonly used sizes are #2 and #3.

Washing a Cleaver: Be sure to wash the cleaver by hand instead of using the dish washer.

To sharpen a cleaver, you can use either a hand sharpener, an electric knife sharpener, or a wet-stone.

THE WOK

The wok is the most important utensil in Chinese cooking. It is a round, concave iron (or stainless steel) skillet, used by the Chinese cook to pan-fry, stir-fry, deep-fry, simmer, stew, or steam. The shape of the wok makes it very retentive of heat, and therefore very economical to use as a cooking utensil.

Originally, woks were made of heavy cast iron. They sat upon iron stands, directly over the burner flame. Cast iron woks are good, because they hold their heat well, and it is almost impossible to wear them out. However, they are too heavy and cumbersome to use in the modern kitchen.

Nowadays, there are available woks made of stainless steel with copper bottoms. These are very light, have a plastic handle, and serve very well for Chinese cooking. This type of wok is very similar to the frying pan. Because it already has a flat bottom, it does not require the metal stand that the older type of wok rests upon.

The question often arises as to which type of fuel is more effective for Chinese cooking--gas or electricity? It has been my experience that there is better control of heat when cooking with a gas flame. Hence, I find gas to be preferable, although electricity may be used.

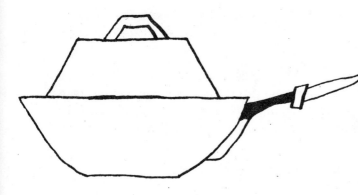

When purchasing a wok, be sure to buy the necessary accessories. These would include a cover, a spatula, a metal rack for supporting the dish used when steam cooking, and a bamboo wire strainer. You may also wish to purchase the ladle, which is used together with the spatula to stir-fry when cooking large quantities.

The wok is indeed versatile, and your success in Chinese cooking will depend in no small measure upon your mastery of the many ways of cooking with the wok.

I wish you Good Luck!

STIR-FRYING

"Stir-fry" is the method most often used in Chinese cooking.

"Chow" is the Chinese translation for "stir-fry". Therefore, when you read a Chinese menu, and you see "chow" as a prefix of one thing or another, you know immediately that it is a stir-fried dish. For example, "chow fan" is stir-fried rice; "chow mein" is stir-fried noodles; and "chow don" is stir-fried eggs.

Stir-fry is essentially heating the wok to a high temperature and adding a small amount of oil, and, if called for by the recipe, the garlic and ginger. Allow these to sizzle and burn a little before you remove them. Then add your main ingredients. Temperature control is critical; it can be too hot, or worse, not hot enough for the food you are handling. A "feel" for the correct temperature will come with your experience in cooking with the wok. (Never add oil when the wok is cold!) Then the ingredients are put into the wok, and constantly stirred about with a spatula. The object is to cook with continuous movement of the food, so that it never cooks overly long on any one part of its surface.

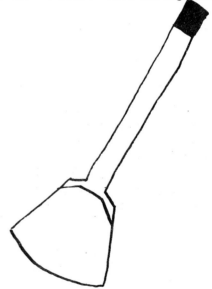

When vegetables are stir-fried, they retain the original color and remain crunchy. They are stir-fried for from 2 to 3 minutes.

You will discover that stir-frying is required for 3 minutes when preparing meat, poultry, and seafood recipes.

STEAMING

"Steaming" is another way to cook with the wok. It is an improvement over boiling, in that foods do not lose their vitamins, juices and flavor to the water. Therefore, steaming is a very healthful way of cooking foods.

In other sections of the book, you will find recipes for steaming eggs, meat cakes, chicken, fish, etc. Do try this method of cooking, as it will most likely be new to you. You will be pleasantly surprised! You will find that steaming left-overs is a marvelous way to re-heat without drying out the food. You will also discover that steaming creates delicious food tastes when steam mingles with the natural juices of pork, chicken, or fish. Chinese children eat entire bowls of rice with not much more than the natural juices from steamed dishes.

To use the wok as a steam-cooker, you need a rack upon which to rest the dish to be cooked. Inexpensive metal racks may be purchased, or you may improvise. Simply remove the top and the bottom from a tin can (such as a tuna can), and use it as a rack. If you don't own a wok, you may use a large covered saucepan.

In all steam-cooked recipes, place the food in a shallow dish or a pie pan. Be sure that the water in the wok is enough to just cover the rack. Bring the water to a boil **before timing** the steaming. Otherwise, you will be under-cooking, and as in steamed eggs, the food will not be done. Of course, you need to cover the food while steaming.

DEEP-FRYING

You will find the wok to be an excellent utensil for deep-frying; however, a regular saucepan will serve the purpose very well if you don't own a wok. A regular frying pan is too shallow for deep-frying as the oil will spatter too much.

Deep-frying requires a Chinese strainer. For example: Put cashew nuts in the strainer while they are deep frying and being removed. This greatly simplifies the process.

Chinese cooks usually test oil temperature by using a chopstick. When you place the chopstick in the hot oil, bubbles will form around the chopstick if the oil is the correct temperature. If the bubbles form very fast, the oil will be too hot. (You may use a cooking thermometer if you wish. The temperature for deep-frying would be 325 - 350 degrees.)

If you are deep-frying meat or poultry and you are uncertain about the correct temperature needed for what you are preparing, test the temperature of the oil with a piece of bread or a thin slice of ginger. The bread or ginger will burn if the oil is too hot. This is also true when deep-frying meat. The outside will burn while the inside remains raw.

Save the oil used for deep-frying as it may be cooled and used for several more times. It should be stored at room temperature.

PAN-FRYING

Another use of the wok is pan-frying. That is, using the wok as a frying pan. But what advantages! Fry an egg in a wok; it will turn out nice and round every time. Fry bacon or hamburger in a wok. The concave shape holds greasy splatter to a minimum. Fry rice, or stir-fry vegetables in the wok; again, the shape of the wok helps to keep all the contents within the utensil.

The technique of pan-frying with the wok is simple. Merely heat the wok, add a teaspoon or two of cooking oil, and proceed as you would with a regular frying pan. When cooking greasy foods such as bacon or hamburger, splatter may be further minimized by the use of a wire screen splatter cover.

The Chinese pan-fry their noodles in the wok. French toast, steaks, chops, chicken, and fish all can be pan-fried this way.

STEWING, ETC.

The next time you make stew or spaghetti try using the wok for the cooking. You will find that there is less loss of the natural juices. The shape of the wok serves to condense the steam and return it to the stew. Because more of the natural juices are retained, you will find your stew or pot roast to be more flavorful! To stew with the wok, merely set it on low heat and cover.

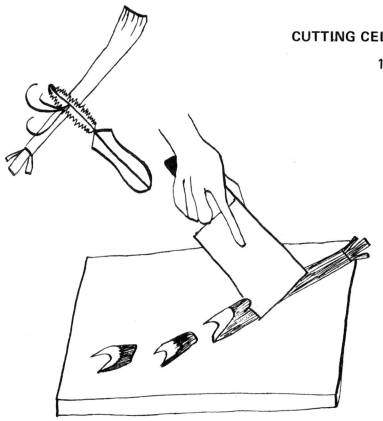

CUTTING CELERY

1. Before cutting celery, use a vegetable peeler and lightly pare away the backs of the celery. This removes the stringy fibres, and you will find that every stalk will taste young and tender.

2. Holding the knife at an angle, cut celery into 1½″ pieces.

3. Cut pieces lengthwise into thin strips.

HOW TO SLIVER GREEN ONIONS

Green onions are used in preparing many Chinese dishes. The entire onion is used. They are diced or slivered, depending upon the dish being prepared. Besides adding flavor, the tops make the dish colorful and attractive.

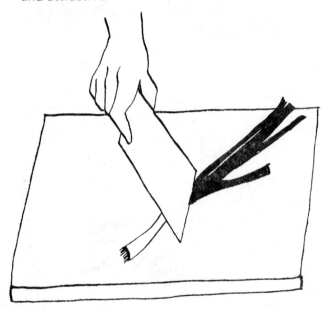

1.   Cut the onion into 1½" lengths.

2.   Cut each piece lengthwise, into slivers.

SLICING FLANK STEAK

Flank steak is the cut most preferred for Chinese cooking. It is flavorful, tender and free of fat. It is also economical, in that one flank steak will serve from 4 to 6 persons, when combined with vegetables and served in the Chinese manner.

You will find that partially freezing the steak will facilitate cutting.

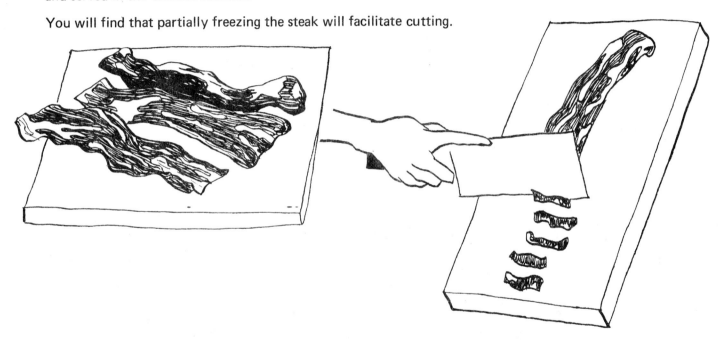

1. Cut steak lengthwise, into three equal strips.

2. Cut each strip crosswise (against the grain) into thin slices.

15

INGREDIENTS USED IN CHINESE COOKING

BAMBOO SHOOTS — Packed in water, or seasoned. Be sure to buy the water packed tips when preparing recipes in this book. Tips are both more tender and more attractive to the eye than the whole bamboo shoots. Remaining bamboo shoot tips will keep in the refrigerator for a week if kept in water. Change water every 2 or 3 days.

BEAN CAKES — Come packed in jars. Keep well under refrigeration. Very pungent, and of soft consistency. Mash with a spoon, add a little sugar, soy sauce, clove of crushed garlic; then spread on meat or fish before steaming. Also used in stir-fry vegetables. Sprinkle one cake with sugar, steam for 1 or 2 minutes and eat as an accompaniment to rice.

BEAN SAUCE — Comes packed in cans. Rinse lightly to reduce salty flavor. When mashed into a paste, use in preparing steamed fish, stir-fried meat, and seafoods. Keeps well up to 2 years under refrigeration.

BEAN SPROUTS — A vegetable sprouted from the soy bean. Resembles the sprout from an old potato. Very delicate but tasty. Cooks in a very short time; easily overcooked. Canned bean sprouts are available, but these are seldom satisfactory. Fresh bean sprouts are very inexpensive.

BLACK BEANS, SALTED — Be careful when purchasing black beans, as there are two types. One is a hard bean, used in soups. The ones we want are the softer beans, labeled "Salty Black Beans". Both kinds come in a similar package, so again, be careful. Salty

INGREDIENTS USED IN CHINESE COOKING

BLACK BEANS, SALTED (Continued—)

black beans are used to provide the indescribable taste of black bean sauce. May be stored in a jar at room temperature for 1 year. To make black bean sauce, the beans are first rinsed once or twice. This removes the excess salt. Do not bother removing the black bean covering that may wash loose. Then place the beans in a deep bowl, and mash them into a paste. Use with a clove of minced garlic as garlic and black beans are always combined to bring out the flavor in preparing spareribs, steamed fish or prawns.

BLACK MUSHROOMS — These mushrooms have a very distinctive flavor. They are available in various sizes, and the cost depends upon the size. Small ones cost less per pound. Dried black mushrooms will keep 2 or 3 years in a cool, dry place.

To use, the mushrooms should be soaked for 30 minutes to an hour in cold water. Or, if in a hurry, boil slowly for 10 minutes. Remove from water, squeeze dry, and cut off the stems of each mushroom with a knife or scissors. Discard the stems.

BOK CHOY — Popular Chinese vegetable, available all year round, and inexpensive. All of the boy choy is edible, including the heart or stalk of the vegetable.

INGREDIENTS USED IN CHINESE COOKING

CHICKEN STOCK — There are many ways to prepare this. Canned chicken broth, chicken base, or bouillon cubes may be used. Use 1 cube of chicken bouillon, or 1 t. chicken base for each 2 cups of water. Or, boil a chicken carcass in 2 quarts of water. Add a slice of fresh ginger root. Bring it to a boil and simmer for ½ hour. Add salt and soy sauce to taste. Strain and store in refrigerator until ready to use. It will keep for several days.

CHINESE SAUSAGES — Pork sausages, flavored and dried for the Oriental taste. These resemble link pork sausages, but are reddish in color. Eaten as an accompaniment to rice, or chopped and used in making meatcakes. Sausages will keep under refrigeration up to 2 months.

CLOUD FUNGUS — Also known as Cloud Ears. A relative of the mushroom. Dark brown, shaped like ears. Very bland in taste, but provide a crunchy texture to vegetable dishes. Must be soaked in warm water for 15 minutes, then rinsed thoroughly before using. They double in size when soaked. Look for these in mushroom section of food stores. Keep indefinitely.

CORNSTARCH — Instead of flour, Chinese cooks utilize cornstarch in their cooking. It is used for thickening gravies, coating meats for marinating, and for making batter for deep-fried foods.

For thickening, use 1 part cornstarch to 2 parts of cold water. Slowly add this mixture to the dish you are preparing and bring it to a boil, stirring constantly (approximately 1 minute). Experiment to find out how much of this cornstarch mixture to use. It takes much less than a flour mixture to achieve the desired result.

Add the cornstarch **AFTER** the soy sauce when marinating meat. This allows the cornstarch to adhere better to the meat.

INGREDIENTS USED IN CHINESE COOKING

DRIED BEAN CURD — Made from yellow soy beans, keeps for many months, and is a good source of protein. Available in two shapes, round and flat. For faster cooking, the flat type is recommended. Both types must be soaked in warm water before using.

EGG ROLL SKINS — Available in one or two pound packages. Contains 16 skins to a pound. To store in refrigerator or freezer, put in a plastic bag so as to retain the moisture. If frozen, allow to thaw for at least several hours before handling. They will keep one week in the refrigerator and about three months if frozen.

FIVE SPICE POWDER — A combination of 5 different spices, packaged and sold in plastic bags. Used sparingly in roasting or stewing meat or poultry.

A flavoring salt made with this powder is used as a condiment for eating deep-fried chicken, duck, or squab. See index for **FLAVORING SALT** recipe. Keeps indefinitely.

FRESH GINGER — GINGER ROOT — Available in any Chinese grocery or super market. Chinese prefer to use the fresh root of ginger, rather than ginger powder, as the fresh root gives a more pungent aroma and taste. Use sparingly. A piece of root will keep for a couple of months in a dry place or in a plastic bag in the refrigerator for several weeks.

GLUTINOUS RICE POWDER — Powder used in preparing dessert dishes. Check label for "glutinous" when purchasing to avoid error.

HOISIN SAUCE — A sweet, reddish sauce, used as a condiment for Pekin Duck. Keep under refrigeration for 2 - 3 years.

19

INGREDIENTS USED IN CHINESE COOKING

LILY FLOWER (dried) — Also known as **GOLDEN NEEDLE**, because of its needle-like shape and golden color. Each needle is about 3" long and must be soaked in warm water for about 10 minutes. Cut off about ½" from the pointed end of each needle, as this part is very tough. You will find them near the dried mushroom section in a Chinese grocery store. Keep indefinitely.

LOTUS ROOT — Tuber of the lotus plant; similar to dahlia tuber. Delicious in soups; crisp texture when stir-fried. When cut crosswise, the pieces have a very lacy design. Cut lengthwise for soup, lotus root will have delicate threads when bitten into. Available in Chinese grocery stores. Will keep 2 weeks in refrigerator. Dried, sweetened lotus roots are sold as a confection. Used to sweeten tea, when it is served for special occasions.

MUSTARD POWDER — When mixing mustard, use equal parts of hot water and mustard. This works better in releasing the essence of the mustard and results in a much **HOTTER** mustard. To make a smooth mustard, add a drop or two of oil to the finished product.

INGREDIENTS USED IN CHINESE COOKING

NAPA CABBAGE — Also known as **CHINESE CELERY CABBAGE;** is a cross between lettuce and "bok choy". It is great for stir-frying with beef, or as a vegetable in soups. Very sweet tasting, and inexpensive.

NOODLES, DEEP-FRIED — "YEE MEIN" are noodles that have already been cooked by deep-frying. They are packaged for sale in plastic bags. Yee Mein may be served in a soup or in gravy. They keep fresh for about 1 month. Purchase in any Oriental market.

NOODLES, FRESH — Sold in 1 lb. plastic bags. Will keep for a week in the refrigerator or several months in freezer. Dried noodles may be substituted for fresh, if fresh ones are not available. Cooking time for dried noodles is approximately double that of the fresh kind. Fresh noodles may be purchased in a Chinese grocery store or frozen ones may be found in the frozen food section of the supermarket.

OIL — When cooking Chinese, use any of the unsaturated free-flowing oils, such as safflower, peanut, or vegetable oil. Chinese cooking never includes butter, although lard is sometimes used.

OYSTER SAUCE — This sauce is a primary ingredient in many of the recipes. It is made from oysters, salt, starch, and caramel coloring. Oyster sauce is very distinctive in flavor, and may be used either in cooking, or as a condiment. It does not have a fishy flavor. It is delicious as a steak sauce. Buy the more expensive brands, as they are definitely superior in flavor. After opening, will keep up to 2 years if refrigerated.

INGREDIENTS USED IN CHINESE COOKING

RED DATES —

Chinese dates, dried for preserving. To use, soak for 10 minutes, remove pits, and check insides for possible rot. Cut dates lengthwise into thin strips, or use whole in soups. Used for their sweet taste, which is imparted to soups and steamed dishes. Keep many months.

RICE —

Two kinds of rice are used in Oriental cooking--the long grain, and the "sweet", or glutinous rice. For every day eating, the Chinese prefer the long grain variety. Raw rice should be rinsed before cooking. For pre-cooked rice, follow package directions.

To measure the amount of water to use in cooking rice, use enough water to cover the rice to a depth of approximately one inch. A good indicator is the first knuckle of your middle finger, when the tip of the finger is resting on the surface of the rice and the water just reaches the knuckle.

RICE STICKS —

"PY MEI FUN" in Chinese. A type of dried noodle, made from rice flour. Rice sticks are used in one of 3 ways; served in soup, in chow mein, or deep-fried. Deep-fry only a small amount at a time, as the rice sticks increase in size. Deep-fry for 2 minutes. When purchasing, do not mistake bean threads for rice sticks, as they are very similar in appearance. Keep indefinitely.

SESAME OIL —

This is a flavoring oil, used to lend zest to cold plates, soups, or noodle dishes. Use sparingly, as a few drops go a long way. Once opened, sesame oil should be stored in the refrigerator, or it will quickly turn rancid.

INGREDIENTS USED IN CHINESE COOKING

SNOW PEAS — Everybodys favorite Chinese vegetable! It is colorful, and has a delicious flavor and pleasing texture. Snow peas are best described as a regular pea pod, but flatter. They are not shelled, as the entire vegetable is eaten. There are stringy threads along each edge of the pea pod, and these are first removed before eating. Remove by snapping off each end of the Snow Pea, then pulling the string down the side (much like unzipping a purse!).

SOY SAUCE — A sauce made from the soy bean, with salt, sugar, flour, and water added. Used in preparing many Chinese dishes, as well as for a condiment. There are two kinds of soy sauce; one is thin and reddish, the other thicker and darker in color. The thin kind is saltier in taste, and is used more for seasoning and marinating. The dark soy sauce is sweeter, not as salty, and similar to the Japanese Kikkoman soy sauce. It is used more for coloring gravies and in frying rice. Because it is not so salty, you may prefer it over the thin soy sauce. Keeps many months at room temperature.

STAR ANISE — An ingredient used to impart a licorice type flavor to foods. Used in cooking much as bay leaf is used in stews. Keeps indefinitely.

23

INGREDIENTS USED IN CHINESE COOKING

TEA —

In China, tea is the beverage commonly found in every home. Instead of water or soda pop, the Chinese home maintains a constant teapot. The tea is made fresh every morning, and then is kept warm throughout the day in either a thermos or an insulated wicker basket. This tea is drunk throughout the day, and when guests drop by, it is properly served to them.

There are many kinds of tea. In addition to their differences in taste, teas are also classified as either "strong" or "mild" teas. The expert tea drinker selects the kind of tea he will drink according to the state of his health. If he is feeling poorly, he will select a milder tea, and avoid the stronger type. For every day use, a milder tea, such as "Oolong" or "Jasmine" is most commonly used. Tea keeps indefinitely; the longer you have it, the better the flavor becomes.

When having "tea lunch" in a restaurant, the Chinese will select a more exotic tea. The waiter always asks "Yum meh chah?", which means, "What kind of tea?" Then "Look On", "Po Nay", or "Li Chee" tea may be ordered.

In order to make good tea, observe the following:

1. Be sure the water is boiling hot, not merely lukewarm.
2. Use 1 t. of tea to each quart of water.
3. Pre-heat the teapot or thermos by running in hot water and rinsing.
4. Put the tea leaves in first, then add the boiling water.
5. Allow tea to steep for at least 5 minutes before serving.

Chinese teas are taken "as is"; sugar, lemon, or cream is NEVER added!

INGREDIENTS USED IN CHINESE COOKING

WATER CHESTNUTS — **Fresh** water chestnuts are imported from Taiwan or Hong Kong. They have the sweetness and texture of a crisp apple. They are very good in won-ton filling, in meat cakes, or in stir-fried vegetable dishes. Peel water chestnuts with a potato peeler, cutting off the top and bottom with a knife or cleaver. Rinse and keep in cold water to prevent discoloration. If refrigerated, will keep fresh for a couple of days. (Unpeeled, they will keep about 2 weeks in the refrigerator.)

Canned water chestnuts come already peeled. The canning process makes these less desirable than the fresh ones. The taste may be improved by stir-frying them in a little oil, adding a small amount of sugar before using in the recipe.

WINE — Wine is used in Chinese cooking of poultry and seafoods. Rice wine or any dry white wine may be used. Wine is used for its flavor, and for cutting the fishy taste of seafoods. Most recipes require only very small amounts of wine. Vegetable dishes never require wine in their preparation.

WINTER MELON — A light green melon, resembling a watermelon, but lightly covered with a fine white powder. Weighs from 10 - 15 lbs. In season and available all year round. Keeps well in cool place for months. May be purchased whole or in pieces. Cut pieces, if refrigerated, will keep for one week. It is used to make **WINTER MELON SOUP.** When dried and sugared, it is used as a confection or used for sweetening tea on special occasions.

WON TON SKINS — One pound contains approximately 80 skins. To store in refrigerator or freezer, put in a plastic bag so as to retain moisture. If frozen, allow to thaw for at least several hours before handling. They will keep one week in the refrigerator and about three months in the freezer.

INGREDIENTS USED IN CHINESE COOKING

WOOD FUNGUS — Also known as **DRIED FUNGUS**. These are larger, and even more crunchy than the cloud ears. Usually used in soups. Soak in warm water at least 30 minutes, then rinse thoroughly before using. Keep indefinitely.

TABLE OF MEASUREMENTS

In this book the following abbreviations have been used:

t.   represents teaspoon (level)

T.   represents tablesoon (level)

C.   represents cup

CHINESE DOUGHNUTS

(Jeen Dui)

Makes approx. 16

DOUGH

½ lb. Chinese brown sugar bars*
1 C. & 2 T. cold water

1 lb. glutinous rice powder

1. Dissolve sugar bar by letting it stand in the water overnight. A quicker method is to dissolve the sugar by using a double boiler over medium heat. **(Use when cool.)**
2. Put the rice powder in a mixing bowl; add sugar syrup and mix well to form a dough.
3. Cover dough with a damp towel until ready to use.

SWEET FILLING

2/3 C. raw or roasted peanuts
1/3 C. raw sesame seeds

2 ozs. candied winter melon, diced
½ C. shredded coconut, sweetened

1. Heat oil to 325 degrees and deep-fry peanuts for 5 minutes. Cool and grind.
2. Toast sesame seeds in a saucepan for 2 minutes, using low heat, no oil, and stirring constantly.
3. Mix all ingredients together.

Note: The sweet filling may be prepared a couple of days in advance and stored in a closed container at room temperature.

*Can be purchased in a Chinese grocery store.

Continued

Chinese Doughnuts (Continued)

MEAT AND SHRIMP FILLING

½ lb.	lean ground pork
20	Chinese mushrooms, small
¼ lb.	fresh prawns
9	water chestnuts, canned
1	green onion, chopped
1 t.	sugar
½ C.	chicken stock
2½ T.	oil

Seasoning for pork:

½ t.	salt
½ t.	sugar
½ t.	thin soy sauce
½ t.	oyster sauce
1 t.	cornstarch

1. Add "seasoning" to pork and mix well.
2. Boil mushrooms for 10 minutes, rinse, squeeze dry, cut off and discard stems; then, chop into very small pieces.
3. Shell, devein, wash, drain and dice prawns.
4. Crush water chestnuts with the flat side of the cleaver.
5. Heat wok, add ½ T. oil and stir-fry water chestnuts for 2 minutes, adding 1 t. sugar. Set aside.
6. Reheat wok, add 1 T. oil and stir-fry prawns, green onion and mushrooms for 3 minutes, lightly sprinkling with salt and sugar. Set aside.
7. Heat wok, add 1 T. oil and stir-fry seasoned pork for 3 minutes.
8. Add chicken stock, cover and cook for 5 minutes. Turn off heat.
9. Add previously prepared ingredients, mix thoroughly and let cool before using.

Note: For doughnuts use either "sweet filling" or "meat and shrimp filling".

Continued

Chinese Doughnuts (Continued)

SHAPING AND FILLING THE DOUGHNUTS

¼ C.   raw sesame seeds   1½ qts.   oil (for deep-frying)

1. Shape dough into rolls about 2'' in diameter.
2. Cut each roll into 1½'' pieces and shape each piece into a very shallow bowl.
3. Put ¾ T. filling in the center; then enclose the filling in the dough, giving the dough a little twist to seal it.
4. Roll doughnuts in sesame seeds.
5. Heat oil to 325 degrees and gently drop in few doughnuts at a time, as they are apt to stick together and **must** be kept separated.
6. When the doughnuts begin to brown and float, which takes about 2 minutes, gently press each one several times with your Chinese strainer while they are frying. This makes the doughnut puffy. Deep-fry for another 6 minutes.
7. Remove doughnuts and place on paper towels to drain.

Note: Jeen Dui is a favorite pastry of the Chinese, usually enjoyed in celebration of the Chinese New Year. They are delicious when eaten hot out of the pot. This is a good example of how Chinese pastry differs from American pastry.

Variation: The dough may be cooked alone, without any filling. Shape into small balls **(1'' in diameter)**, or 1½'' x ½'' cigar shapes, and fry as above.

CHINESE FRIED DUMPLINGS
(Jow Gwok Jai)

Makes approx. 80

1 pkg. round dumpling skins*
¼ C. sesame seeds
½ C. raw peanuts (roasted may be used)
4 slices candied winter melon, diced
½ C. shredded coconut (sweetened)

1½ t. sugar
2 egg whites
2 qts. oil, for deep-frying

1. Toast the raw sesame seeds in a skillet or frying pan over medium-low flame for 3 minutes, using no oil. Stir frequently to prevent burning.

2. Heat oil to 325 degrees and deep-fry peanuts for 5 minutes. (**If roasted peanuts are used, omit this step.**)

3. When cool, grind peanuts in food grinder, or chop into bits with cutting knife.

4. Mix all the ingredients together, **EXCEPT** egg whites.

5. Make dumplings by putting 1 t. of the filling mixture onto each dumpling skin. Moisten edge of skin with egg white, fold dumpling in half, and seal the edges by pressing firmly together with your fingers.

6. Heat oil to 350 degrees and deep-fry dumplings for 3 minutes. Turn and fry opposite side for 2 minutes, until light golden brown. Remove and drain on paper towels.

Note: Fried dumplings are a Chinese goodie that is usually prepared and served during the New Year Celebration. They will keep nicely in a closed container for 3 or 4 days.

*Dumpling skins are similar to **WON TON** skins--except that they are round and slightly thinner. You may substitute **WON TON** skins by merely cutting off the corners to round off the skins; or, use **WON TON** skins and fold into a triangle.

EGG ROLLS
(Choon Guen)

1 pkg.	egg roll skins (32)		½ t.	salt
½ lb.	barbecued pork OR 2 C. cooked		½ t.	sugar
	chicken or ham		1¼ t.	thin soy sauce
2	stalks celery		1½ T.	oyster sauce
4	green onions		2 T.	oil
½ can	bamboo shoot tips*		1 qt.	oil for deep-frying
1 can	sliced mushrooms, 3 ozs.		2	egg whites for sealing skins
1 lb.	fresh bean sprouts			
¼ lb.	raw prawns			

1. Cut the pork, celery, onions, and bamboo shoots into thin strips (julienne style), about 2" long.

2. Shell, devein, wash and drain prawns. Cut into thin strips.

3. Heat wok, add 1 T. oil. Then add the celery, bean sprouts and green onions with ½ t. salt, ½ t. sugar. Stir-fry for 2 minutes; then set aside in a dish.

4. In hot wok, add 1 t. oil. Stir-fry bamboo shoots, barbecued pork and mushrooms for 2 minutes. Set aside.

5. Now in hot wok, with 1 t. oil, stir-fry the prawns for 2 minutes. Sprinkle lightly with salt, sugar and ¼ t. thin soy sauce.

6. Remove wok from fire. Combine ingredients (previously set aside) in the wok with the prawns. Add the oyster sauce and the remaining 1 t. of thin soy sauce.

7. Mix all ingredients thoroughly by tossing with spatula or large spoon. With a spoon, remove all liquid that has collected in bottom of the wok. If this is not done, your egg rolls will be SOGGY!

8. Wrap egg rolls, using 2 tablespoonful of filling per egg roll. See diagram on following page.

9. Heat oil to 325 degrees and deep-fry egg rolls for 6 minutes, 3 minutes on each side. Remove and drain on paper towels.

Serving Suggestions: Egg rolls may be served as hors d'oeuvres, or as part of a multi-course dinner. Sprinkle egg rolls lightly with worcestershire sauce or serve small quantities of hot mustard and catsup as condiments.

*Buy water packed bamboo shoot tips in 15 oz. can.

HOW TO WRAP AN EGG ROLL

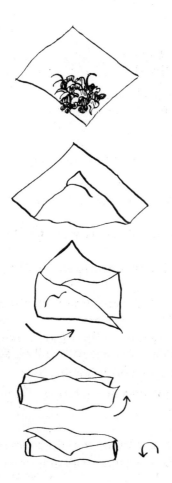

1. With one corner of the skin toward you, place 2 T. filling about 2" from the corner.

2. Fold that corner so that the point is about 1½" from the opposite corner.

3. Fold as an envelope, leaving it about 4" long.

4. Roll it twice, to form a cylinder.

5. Moisten the corner with egg white; seal.

SHRIMP BALLS
(Ha Kau)

Makes 45

2	slices white bread
2 T.	cold chicken stock
1 lb.	raw prawns
6	fresh water chestnuts (or canned)*
1	green onion, chopped
2	slices bacon OR 1½ ozs. pork fat (NOT salt pork)
1 qt.	oil for deep-fry

"A"

1 t.	salt
½ t.	sugar
½ t.	thin soy sauce
½ t.	oyster sauce
1	egg
1½ T.	cornstarch

1. Crumble and soak bread in the chicken stock.

2. Shell, devein, wash and drain prawns.

3. Peel fresh water chestnuts. **(Canned ones come peeled.)** Crush with the flat side of the cleaver. Chop fine if you don't have a cleaver.

4. Boil pork fat for 5 minutes in 1½ C. boiling water. Drain and dice. If you use bacon, omit the boiling step and just dice it.

5. Place prawns, pork fat **(or bacon)**, water chestnuts and onion on the chopping board. Chop and mix until they are minced. Place in a large bowl.

6. Add ingredients listed under "A" to the prawn mixture. Mix thoroughly with the bread and chicken stock mixture.

7. Form into balls about 1¼" in diameter.

8. Heat oil to 325 degrees and deep-fry shrimp balls for 6 minutes, 3 minutes on each side. Remove and drain on paper towels.

Note: Shrimp balls may be pan-fried like little pancakes 2" in diameter and ¼" thick. Fry 6 or 7 at a time in a small amount of oil until they are golden brown--about 3 - 4 minutes on each side.

Serving Suggestions: Serve as appetizers or as one of the dishes in a Chinese dinner.

*If you use canned water chestnuts, crush and stir-fry them in 1 t. oil for 1 - 2 minutes, adding 1 t. sugar. Let cool before using.

SHRIMP TOAST
(Ha Doh See)

Serves 4 - 6

¼ lb.	fresh prawns		1	egg white (small egg)
¼	yellow onion, chopped		½ t.	salt
1	green onion, chopped		¼ t.	sugar
4 - 5	slices bread		¼ t.	thin soy sauce
4 T.	oil			dash of pepper
			1½ T.	cornstarch

1. Shell, devein, wash, drain and mince prawns. Place in a mixing bowl.

2. Add egg white, salt, sugar, soy sauce, dash of pepper, both kinds of onion and cornstarch to the prawns and mix well.

3. Remove crust from bread slices; toast lightly. Cut each slice into 4 triangles, by making two diagonal cuts.

4. Spread shrimp mixture generously on each toast triangle.

5. Heat wok or frying pan. Add 2 T. oil and fry the shrimp side of the toast for 3 minutes over medium-low heat. Turn and fry opposite side for 2 minutes.

6. Repeat this procedure with the remaining shrimp toast.

Note: This is a delicious hors d'oeuvres for any occasion, or snack for afternoon or evening.

BASIC NOODLE SOUP
(Tong Mein)

Serves 4

1½ qts.	water
½ lb.	fresh noodles (or dried noodles)
4 C.	chicken stock
½ t.	thin soy sauce
1	green onion, chopped (for garnish)

1. In a large container bring water to a boil, add noodles and cook for 3 minutes. (**If you use dried noodles, cook for 5 minutes.**) Drain in colander, run under cold water, and drain again.

2. Bring chicken stock to a boil, add soy sauce and noodles; then, bring it to a fast boil.

3. Serve in individual bowls, garnishing with the chopped green onion.

Serving Suggestions: Serve with **OYSTER BEEF** or **STIR-FRY BOK CHOY**;

Vary the Noodle Soup Dish by adding:
Oyster Beef
Cashew Chicken
Chinese Barbecued Pork
Pan-fried Eggs
Sliced Hard-boiled Egg
Left-over roasted chicken
Left-over roasted pork

BIRD'S NEST SOUP
(Yin Wau Tong)

Serves 8

3 ozs. Bird's Nest (½ box)
1   chicken, 2 to 3 lbs.
4 qts. water
1 piece fresh ginger root, (approx. 1" thick), crushed
1 t.   salt

1. Soften nests by boiling in 2 qts. of water for 10 minutes. Drain and rinse with cold water. Clean by removing all feathers while nest is suspended in water. (All package directions may be disregarded when following this recipe).

2. Remove skin from chicken, cut and quarter.

3. Bring 4 qts. of water to a boil. Add all remaining ingredients (except salt) to the boiling water and cover. Cook over medium heat for 3 hours.

4. Remove and cool the chicken. After removing the flesh from the carcass, cut or tear the chicken into edible size pieces and put back into the soup.

5. Add salt, and serve.

Note: After preparation, this soup may be kept under refrigeration for several days until ready to use.

Serving Suggestion: Finely chopped green onion and ham may be used as garnish on top of soup to serve to company.

Interesting Information!

Bird's Nest Soup is one of China's great delicacies. It is made from the jelly-like substance that swallows extrude from their mouths to build their nests. The nests are collected after the swallows have abandoned them and are then thoroughly washed and cleaned. Next they are sterilized with sulphur fumes. Finally, they are dried and packaged for export.

Packaged bird's nests will keep indefinitely!

CHICKEN MEATBALL SOUP
(Gai Kau Tong)

Serves 4

½ lb.   chicken meat
¾ C.   frozen peas, defrosted*
4 C.   water
½ t.   chicken base (or 1 chicken bouillon cube)
1   egg

SEASONING
½ t. salt
½ t. sugar
½ t. thin soy sauce
1 t. cornstarch
     dash of pepper

1. Remove skin and bones from chicken. Mince finely with cleaver.
2. Add "seasoning" to chicken meat and mix thoroughly.
3. Bring water to a boil. Form small balls with the chicken mixture and drop into the boiling water. **(Should make about 14 balls).** Cover and simmer over medium heat for 7 minutes.
4. Now add the peas and simmer for 2 more minutes.
5. Add the chicken base or bouillon. **(May be omitted if you prefer to salt to your taste.)**
6. Beat raw egg and add to the soup as it boils.

Note: This is a quick soup that may be prepared within 15 minutes if all ingredients are prepared ahead of time.

Variations: This recipe can be varied by using lean ground pork, or fresh shelled prawns in place of chicken.

*Fresh peas may be substituted.

CHICKEN WHISKEY SOUP
(Gai Jau Tong)

Serves 4

1 lb. chicken parts
4 dried red dates
10 small Chinese mushrooms
14 lily flower needles
10 dried fungus (wood ears)*
1 T. oil
5 C. water
1 T. whiskey
1 t. sugar

SEASONING
½ t. salt
½ t. sugar
½ t. thin soy sauce
  dash of pepper
5 thin slices fresh ginger root

1. Chop chicken into 1½" x ½" pieces.
2. Add "seasoning" to chicken and mix well.
3. Soak dried dates, mushrooms and lily flower needles in separate containers for 20 minutes. Rinse well. Squeeze moisture out of mushrooms and lily flowers.
4. Soak dried fungus for 15 minutes, then rinse thoroughly.
5. Remove seeds from dates and cut into small pieces.
6. Remove and discard mushroom stems. Cut mushrooms into strips, julienne style.
7. Cut off ½" from pointed end of lily flower needles. Discard ends, then cut each needle in half.
8. Heat wok, add oil and stir-fry chicken for 3 minutes.
9. Add water and all other ingredients. Bring it to a boil. Cover and simmer over medium heat for 15 minutes. Serve.

*There are two kinds of dried fungus - cloud ears and wood ears. Cloud ears are soft and are usually used for steaming or for stir-frying. Wood ears are crunchy and usually used in soups.

EGG FLOWER SOUP
(Gai Don Tong)

Serves 4

½ lb. lean ground beef
3 C. chicken stock
½ C. frozen peas, defrosted
1 egg

SEASONING
¼ t. salt
¼ t. sugar
1 t. thin soy sauce
1 t. cornstarch

1. Add "seasoning" to ground beef and mix thoroughly.

2. Bring chicken stock to a boil.

3. Add beef, stirring to separate meat into small pieces; then add the green peas. Cover and cook for 2 minutes.

4. Beat egg well and slowly stir it into the soup. Serve immediately.

Serving Suggestion: Serve with **SOY SAUCE CHICKEN WINGS, PORK SPARERIBS WITH BLACK BEAN SAUCE** and **STEAMED RICE.**

HOT AND SOUR SOUP
(Sheun Lot Tong)

Serves 4

1	whole chicken breast
10	small Chinese mushrooms
15	pieces lily flower (golden needles)
1 C.	dried bean curd*
20	pieces cloud ear
2	dried chili peppers
4 C.	water
1 T.	wine vinegar (tarragon flavoring)
1	egg
½	bouillon cube or ½ t. salt

SEASONING

¼ t. salt
¼ t. sugar
¾ t. thin soy sauce
      dash of pepper
1 t. cornstarch

THICKENING

1½ T. cornstarch
3 T. cold water
1½ t. dark soy sauce
1 t. sugar

1. Cut chicken meat into strips, julienne style; add ingredients listed under "Seasoning" and mix well.
2. Soak mushrooms and lily flowers in separate containers for 20 minutes. Rinse and squeeze dry.
3. Remove and discard mushroom stems. Cut mushrooms into strips, julienne style.
4. Cut about ½" off the pointed end of each lily flower needle. Discard the pointed ends and cut each needle in half.
5. Break dried bean curd into small pieces. Soak in cold water for 15 minutes and drain.
6. Soak cloud ears for 15 minutes (use separate bowl). Rinse thoroughly.
7. Put chili peppers in pot, add water and bring it to a boil.
8. Add chicken, mushrooms, lily flowers and dried bean curd. Cook for 10 minutes in a covered pot.
9. Add cloud ears and vinegar. Cook for 5 minutes more. Then remove chili peppers.
10. Mix ingredients listed under "Thickening" and stir into soup. Cook for 1 more minute.

*Be sure to buy **pieces** of bean curd as the round ones take too long to cook.

Continued

11. Beat the egg, add it to the soup and bring it to a fast boil.
12. Add bouillon cube **OR** ½ t. salt, and serve.

Variation: Use ¼ t. pepper instead of dried chili peppers, and substitute 1 T. apple cider vinegar for the wine vinegar.

LETTUCE SOUP
(Tsang Choy Tong)

Serves 4

¾ lb.   lettuce
¼ lb.   lean ground pork
4 C.   water
½ t.   chicken base
       (or ½ chicken bouillon cube)

SEASONING

½ t. salt
½ t. sugar
¾ t. thin soy sauce
1 t. cornstarch

1. Wash lettuce and break into 2" pieces.

2. Mix ingredients listed under "Seasoning" with the ground pork.

3. Bring water to boil. Add chicken base and the ground pork. **(Drop the meat into the water as little meat balls.)** Cover and cook for 8 minutes.

4. Add the lettuce and cook uncovered for 2 minutes longer; then serve.

Note: This is a delicious soup which can be quickly prepared, with a minimum of ingredients. It is one of the old standbys in a Chinese kitchen.

LOTUS ROOT SOUP
(Lin Ngau Tong)

1 lb.	lotus root*	3	dried red dates
1 lb.	lean pork	4 qts.	water
1 oz.	dried octopus (optional)**		

1. Separate the lotus root by snapping off each tuber. Cut off ends of each tuber; discard.
2. Peel lotus root with a vegetable peeler.
3. Wash octopus.
4. Remove and discard seeds from red dates; wash dates.
5. Put water in a large pot, add octopus, red dates, lotus root and pork. Cover and bring to a boil. Cook for 2½ hours over medium-low heat.
6. Remove the lotus roots, cut in rectangular pieces and put back in the soup.
7. Salt to taste before serving

Note: This is a soup with an indescribably delicious and unusual flavor! You will be delighted with its taste!

*Lotus root may be purchased in a Chinese vegetable store.

**Dried octopus keeps indefinitely and may be purchased in a Chinese grocery store.

BASIC RICE SOUP (Congee)
(Jook)

Serves 6

1¼ C.	rice	1	piece 2" diameter, dried orange peel, optional
¾ t.	salt		
1 t.	oil	½ C.	raw peanuts
5 qts.	water	2 C.	flat bean curd*
4	chicken backs OR	1 t.	salt
1 lb.	neck bones		

1. Wash rice 4 times and drain well. Add ¾ t. salt and the oil to the rice. Let stand at room temperature overnight. **(This makes the soup very smooth!)**

2. Put the water in a large pot along with the chicken backs and orange peel. Cover and bring to a boil.

3. Add rice and raw peanuts and bring to a boil again, uncovered. Then cover, turn heat to medium-low and simmer for 2½ hours. **Be sure to stir frequently** so that it doesn't burn.

4. Break the bean curd into small pieces **(average size 1½" x 1½".)** Soak for 20 minutes and drain well.

5. Add bean curd and cook for 10 minutes.

6. Now add 1 t. salt or salt to taste.

   Garnish with . . . . .
   1. Chopped green onion
   2. Ginger root (½" piece) peeled, thinly sliced and cut julienne style.
   3. Cut abalone julienne style. For variety, you can put the abalone in the bowl and pour the hot soup over it.

*Be sure to buy **pieces** of bean curd as the round ones take too long to cook.

RICE SOUP WITH BEEF
(Ngow Yuk Jook)

1 lb. flank steak	½ t. sugar
1 t. thin soy sauce	1 t. oyster sauce
2 t. white wine	1 T. cornstarch
1 t. salt	dash of pepper

1. Prepare Basic Rice Soup. **(See Page 44)**
2. Cut flank steak **(with the grain)** into 1½'' strips; then cut across the grain into very thin slices.
3. Season meat with remaining ingredients, drop the meat into the hot rice soup, and cook for 10 minutes.

RICE SOUP WITH CHICKEN
(Gai Kau Jook)

6 chicken breasts	dash of pepper
¾ t. salt	1½ t. thin soy sauce
½ t. sugar	1 T. cornstarch

1. Prepare Basic Rice Soup. **(See Page 44)**
2. Skin and bone chicken. **(Bones can be used in making the basic soup!)** Cut chicken into pieces 1½'' x ¾'' x ¼'' thick.
3. Season the chicken with remaining ingredients, drop the chicken into the hot rice soup, and cook for 10 minutes.

RICE SOUP WITH PORK MEATBALLS
(Gee Yuk Jook)

¼ lb.	fresh prawns		½ t.	sugar
¾ lb.	ground pork			dash of pepper
1	green onion, chopped		1 t.	cornstarch
1 t.	thin soy sauce		1 t.	water
1 t.	salt			

1. Prepare Basic Rice Soup. **(See Page 44)**
2. Shell, devein and wash prawns. Dice into very fine pieces.
3. Mix pork, prawns and green onion together.
4. Add soy sauce, salt, sugar, pepper, cornstarch and water in that order.
5. Form into small meat balls, and drop them into the hot rice soup. Cook for 10 minutes.

SEAWEED SOUP
(Gee Choy Tong)

Serves 5

½ lb.   lean pork
2   bean cakes*
3   sheets dried seaweed
5 C.   chicken stock

SEASONING

½ t. salt
½ t. sugar
½ t. thin soy sauce
1 t. cornstarch

1. Cut pork into pieces, 1" x 1½".
2. Add "seasoning" to pork and mix well.
3. Cut each bean cake into 9 squares.
4. Wet seaweed in cold water. Break each sheet into 4 pieces.
5. Bring chicken stock to a boil, and add pork. Cover and cook over medium heat for 10 minutes.
6. Add bean cakes and cook for 3 more minutes.
7. Add seaweed, bring to a fast boil, and serve!

*Buy **firm** kind of bean cake for cooking. Remaining bean cake can be kept in the refrigerator for 3 days.

SIZZLING RICE SOUP
(Woh Bah Tong)

Serves 4

2 C.	hot cooked rice*
¼ lb.	raw prawns
½ C.	frozen peas, defrosted
4 C.	chicken stock
1½ C.	oil

SEASONING

½ t.	salt
½ t.	sugar
½ t.	thin soy sauce
1 t.	cornstarch
	dash of pepper

1. Press hot cooked rice into a thin layer **(about ¼" or less)** on a cookie sheet or any kind of a flat pan. Bake at 350 degrees for 1 hour. **(This may be done a day or two ahead.)** Break the rice into 3" squares and place in a closed container.

2. Shell, devein and wash prawns; then dice and flavor with the ingredients listed under "Seasoning".

3. Bring chicken stock to a boil. Add prawns and the defrosted peas and bring it to a boil again.

4. Heat oil to 325 degrees and deep-fry rice for 5 minutes or until golden brown. Drain.

5. Pour soup in a deep serving bowl and immediately put in the deep-fried rice.
   CAUTION: The soup and rice must both be done at the same time or there won't be a sizzle!

Note: For 'Show' effect, perform Step 5 at the table, in front of your guests.

Serving Suggestion: This soup goes well with **BEEF IN HOISIN SAUCE** and **CURRIED CHICKEN WITH POTATO.**

*Use Japanese rice for this recipe. It is cooked the same way as steamed rice.

WATERCRESS SOUP
(Sai Yong-Choy Tong)

Serves 4

1 bunch watercress
½ chicken breast (about 4 ozs.)
4 C. chicken stock

SEASONING

¼ t. salt
¼ t. sugar
¼ t. thin soy sauce
1 t. cornstarch
dash of pepper

1. Thoroughly rinse watercress, removing any brown leaves.

2. Skin and bone chicken breast, then cut into 1'' pieces.

3. Add "seasoning" to chicken and mix well.

4. Bring the chicken stock to a boil; then add chicken meat and watercress. Cover and simmer for 10 minutes over medium heat. Serve.

WINTER MELON SOUP
(Doong Gwah Tong)

1 pkg.	chicken thighs (approx. 10 ozs.)
½ lb.	winter melon
7 C.	water
6	fresh water chestnuts, peel and dice
½ C.	sliced mushrooms (canned)
½ t.	chicken base (or ½ chicken bouillon cube)

MARINADE

1 t.	salt
½ t.	sugar
½ t.	thin soy sauce
1 t.	cornstarch

1. Remove the meat from the chicken thighs; save the bones for soup. Dice the chicken into small cubes (**approximately ½"**).

2. Sprinkle chicken with each of the ingredients listed under "marinade", mix well and marinate for ½ hour.

3. Remove skin and dice winter melon (**½" cubes**).

4. Measure the water into a large pot, add the chicken bones and boil for 25 minutes.

5. Remove bones from pot, add the chicken and the diced winter melon, cover and cook over medium heat for 10 minutes.

6. Now, add diced water chestnuts, sliced mushrooms and the chicken base or chicken bouillon cube.

7. Bring to a boil, and serve!

Note: The Chinese customarily serve this soup as the first course of a dinner.

The above version of **WINTER MELON SOUP** is simplified. Traditional **WINTER MELON SOUP** required the entire melon, to which the above ingredients are added. Then the soup is produced by steaming the entire melon in a cauldron for 3 to 4 hours. The soup thus produced consists of a flavorful blend of the added ingredients and the native juice of the melon.

BEAN SAUCE CHICKEN
(Min See Gai)

Serves 4

1	whole chicken breast (approx. 12 ozs.)
1	green onion
1	medium size carrot, diced
10	canned water chestnuts, diced
1 T.	bean sauce (canned)
1½ T.	oil
½ t.	sugar
½ C.	water

SEASONING

½ t.	salt
½ t.	sugar
1 t.	thin soy sauce
1 t.	white wine
1 t.	cornstarch

1. Skin and bone chicken. Cut into ¾'' cubes.
2. Add "seasoning" and mix well.
3. Cut green onion into ½'' lengths.
4. Rinse bean sauce once and mash with the handle of the cleaver.
5. Heat wok, add ½ T. oil and stir-fry water chestnuts for 1 minute, adding the ½ t. sugar. Remove and set aside.
6. Reheat wok, add 1 T. oil, bean sauce, chicken, carrot and green onion. Stir-fry for 3 minutes.
7. Add water and bring mixture to a boil, cover and cook for 4 minutes over medium heat.
8. Add water chestnuts, mix well, and serve.

Serving Suggestion: Serve with **TOMATO BEEF CHOW MEIN, SHRIMP BALLS** and **STEAMED RICE.**

BOILED CHICKEN, CANTONESE
(Bok Cheet Gai)

Serves 8

3 - 3½ lbs.   chicken
4 qts.   water
1   piece fresh ginger root
   (about ½"), crushed

1   green onion, whole
2   green onions, slivered (garnish)
1 t.   salt

1.   Clean chicken, being sure to remove all pin-feathers.

2.   Bring water to a boil in a large pot.

·3.   Add ginger, 1 green onion and chicken; put the chicken on its back in the pot. Immediately turn heat to low. Simmer for 15 minutes; then turn the chicken on its breast and cook another 15 minutes. Next, turn it on one side for 15 minutes; then, turn it on the other side for 15 minutes. **(In this way all parts of the chicken will be cooked.)**

4.   Remove chicken from the pot and put it in a large bowl. Run under cold water for 1 - 2 minutes. Remove from the cold water and sprinkle it with the 1 t. salt.   Then, put the chicken back in the bowl of cold water for 1 hour to cool. **(This makes the chicken skin crispy!)**

5.   Chop into serving pieces **(about 30 pieces).**
6.   Garnish with the two slivered green onions. It can be served with hot mustard and oyster sauce.

Variations: **To vary this recipe for company,** arrange the chopped chicken neatly in the center of a large platter and surround the cold chicken with one of the following:

   I.   With Bok Choy **(1 lb.)**

      1.   Break branches off center stock of bok choy, removing and discarding any flowers.

      2.   Peel outer covering off center stock; then cut diagonally into 2" pieces.

      3.   Cut off and discard ¼" from the stem end of each leaf where it was attached to the center stock. Then, cut stems and leaves into 2" lengths.

      4.   Heat wok, add 1 T. oil and stir-fry bok choy for 3 minutes, adding ¾ t. salt and ¾ t. sugar.

Continued

Boiled Chicken, Cantonese (Continued)

5. Add ½ C. chicken stock made from boiling the chicken, and 1 t. dark soy sauce. Bring it to a boil.

6. Make thickening, using 1 T. cornstarch with 2 T. cold water. Add to bok choy and cook for 1 minute more.

7. Remove from wok and arrange bok choy so that it surrounds the cold chicken.

II. With Snow Peas (30)

1. Remove tips and strings from the snow peas. Then cut diagonally into 2 pieces.

2. Heat wok, add 2 t. oil, and stir-fry snow peas for 3 minutes, adding ¼ t. salt, ¼ t. sugar, ½ t. dark soy sauce and ¼ C. chicken stock. Bring it to a boil.

3. Make thickening using 1 t. cornstarch and 2 t. cold water. Add to snow peas and cook for 1 minute.

4. Remove from wok and arrange the snow peas so that they surround the cold chicken.

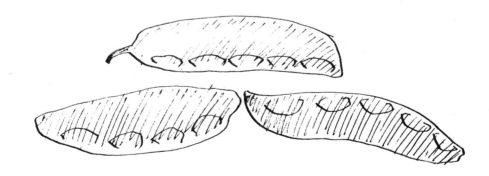

CASHEW NUT CHICKEN
(Yiu Gwoh Gai)

Serves 8

2 - 3 lbs.	chicken or 2 whole chicken breasts
¼ lb.	raw cashew nuts
20	small Chinese mushrooms or 1 medium-size can mushrooms
4	stalks celery
½	can bamboo shoot tips*
15	water chestnuts, fresh or canned
1	yellow onion, thinly sliced
3 T.	oil, approximately
½ t.	salt
½ t.	sugar
2 C.	chicken stock
1 T.	cornstarch
2 T.	water

MARINADE

¾ t.	salt
½ t.	sugar
1 t.	thin soy sauce
1 T.	oyster sauce
	dash of pepper
1 T.	cornstarch

- -

2	green onions, slivered
3	thin slices ginger root, slivered

- -

2 C.	oil for deep-frying

1. Skin and bone chicken. Cut into 2" x ½" pieces.
2. Sprinkle the chicken with each of the ingredients listed under "marinade", mix well and then add the green onions and ginger. Marinate for 1 hour.
3. Heat 2 C. oil to 325 degrees and deep-fry cashew nuts for 5 minutes, drain and salt lightly.
4. Boil Chinese mushrooms for 10 minutes, rinse, squeeze dry, cut off and discard stems. If you use canned mushrooms, omit this step.
5. Cut celery into 1½" pieces, then cut each piece lengthwise into strips, julienne style.
6. Cut bamboo shoot tips into thin slices.

*Buy a 15 oz. can.

Continued

Cashew Nut Chicken (Continued)

7. Peel water chestnuts **(using potato peeler)** and cut a little off the top and the bottom of each one. Then cut them into thin slices and soak in water to prevent them from turning dark. **(Canned water chestnuts are already peeled.)**

8. Heat wok, add 1 t. oil and stir-fry the bamboo tips and water chestnuts together, if you use fresh water chestnuts. **(If canned ones are used, stir-fry them separately in 1 t. oil for 1 - 2 minutes, adding 2 t. sugar.)** Set aside.

9. Heat wok, add 1 t. oil and stir-fry mushrooms, celery and yellow onion for 3 minutes with ½ t. salt and ½ t. sugar. Set aside.

10. Heat wok, add 2 T. oil and stir-fry marinated chicken for 3 minutes. Add chicken stock, cover and cook for 10 minutes over medium heat.

11. Add vegetables which have been previously set aside and bring to a fast boil.

12. Thicken with a mixture made with the cornstarch and 2 T. cold water. Bring to a boil, cook for 1 minute and turn off the heat.

13. Add cashew nuts, mix thoroughly, and serve.

Note: Except for the chicken, you can do all the other stir-frying without oil if you use a teflon fry pan.

The cashew nuts may be deep-fried a couple of days before-hand.

CASHEW NUT CHICKEN may be prepared a few hours in advance and reheated just before serving. Omit the nuts until serving time.

Serving Suggestions: This is a tasty dish that may be served alone or it may be served over rice to make a simple plate dinner or lunch. It also may be served as one of the dishes in a Chinese dinner.

CHICKEN WITH ASPARAGUS
(Lee Sun Gai Kau)

Serves 6

1 lb.	chicken thighs
1½ lbs.	fresh asparagus
1½ T.	black beans
1	clove garlic, crushed
3 T.	oil
½ t.	salt
1 t.	sugar
¾ C.	water
¾ T.	cornstarch
1½ T.	cold water

SEASONING

1 t.	salt
1 t.	sugar
1 t.	thin soy sauce
1	green onion, slivered
	dash of pepper

1. Bone and remove skin from chicken. Cut into 1" x 1½" pieces.
2. Add "seasoning" to chicken and mix well.
3. Cut off and discard the last 2" at the base end of the asparagus. Then, cut each spear diagonally into 2" lengths. Wash and drain.
4. Wash black beans thoroughly **(at least 2 rinses)**. Mash the beans and mix with the crushed garlic.
5. Heat wok. Add 2 T. oil. Stir-fry the seasoned chicken for 5 minutes. Set aside.
6. Reheat wok. Add 1 T. oil and the black bean mixture and cook for 1 minute.
7. Add the asparagus and stir-fry for 2 minutes. Then add salt, sugar, and water.
8. Add the chicken and bring the mixture to a boil.
9. Thicken with cornstarch mixture **(made with ¾ T. cornstarch and 1½ T. cold water)**. Cook for 1 minute, and serve.

Note: This recipe utilizes **FRESH** asparagus. Canned asparagus will not do.

CHICKEN WITH BEAN CAKE SAUCE
(Foo Yueh Gai)

Serves 4

2 lbs.   chicken
2   green onions
2   cloves garlic, crushed
2 T.   bean cake (in jar)*
2 T.   oil
1 T.   cornstarch
2 T.   cold water

½ t.   salt
1 t.   sugar
1 T.   thin soy sauce
1 T.   white wine
1 C.   water
       dash of pepper

1. Chop chicken into 1½" x ½" pieces.

2. Cut green onions into 1" pieces.

3. Heat wok, add oil, garlic and green onions. Stir-fry for ½ minute.

4. Add bean cake and chicken. Stir-fry for 3 minutes.

5. Add all remaining ingredients, **except** cornstarch and 2 T. cold water. Cover and cook for 10 minutes over medium-high heat.

6. Prepare thickening by mixing the cornstarch with 2 T. cold water. Stir it into the chicken and cook for 1 minute, and serve.

Serving Suggestions: **TOMATO BEEF, DICED WINTER MELON SOUP** and **STEAMED RICE** would make a complete dinner. However, when this dish is served over rice, it makes a tasty one-dish lunch or dinner.

Variations: I.   You may substitute pork, cut julienne style, in place of chicken. It should be cooked for 10 minutes.

II.   If you use spareribs in place of chicken, cook the meat for 35 minutes. Use 2 C. water instead of 1 C. **(For cutting the spareribs, see BLACK BEAN SAUCE SPARERIBS.)**

*Bean cake will keep in the refrigerator for a year or so.

57

CHICKEN WITH CABBAGE
(Gai Chow Yeh Choy)

Serves 5

1 lb.	cabbage
2¼ lbs.	chicken
1	green onion, slivered
2 T.	oil
½ t.	salt
½ t.	sugar
¾ C.	chicken stock
1	can sliced mushrooms (4 ozs.)

SEASONING

1 t.	salt
½ t.	sugar
1 t.	thin soy sauce
1 t.	oyster sauce
	dash of pepper

THICKENING

1 T.	cornstarch
½ T.	dark soy sauce
2 T.	cold water

1. Wash cabbage; cut into 1½" x 1½" pieces.

2. Bone the chicken. Remove skin and discard. Cut chicken into 1½" x 1½" pieces. Add "seasoning" and green onion to the chicken and mix well.

3. Heat wok. Add 1 T. oil. Stir-fry cabbage for 3 minutes with ½ t. salt and ½ t. sugar. Remove to dish and set aside.

4. Reheat wok. Add 1 T. oil. Stir-fry chicken for 3 minutes; then add chicken stock and mushrooms. Cook for 5 minutes longer.

5. Now add the cabbage to the chicken. Bring to a fast boil.

6. Combine ingredients listed under "thickening". Stir into the chicken and cabbage mixture; cook for 1 minute, and serve.

Serving Suggestion: Serve over rice as a plate lunch or dinner.

CHICKEN SALAD, CANTONESE
(Sau See Gai)

3 lbs.	chicken
½ C.	raw peanuts
3 ozs.	rice sticks (Py mei fun)
¼ C.	raw sesame seeds
20	snow peas (optional)
3	stalks celery
¼	head lettuce, shredded
3	green onions, slivered
1 T.	oil

- -

1 qt.	oil for deep-frying

"A" SPICES FOR CHICKEN

1 t.	salt
½ t.	sugar
1 t.	thin soy sauce
1 t.	oyster sauce
¼ t.	five spice powder

"B" SPICES FOR SALAD

½ t.	dry mustard
1 t.	water
½ t.	sugar
1 t.	flavored salt*
2 t.	oyster sauce
1 T.	sesame oil

1. Apply spices listed under "A" to the skin and the cavity of the chicken.
2. Roast chicken for 1 hr. 45 min. at 375 degrees (**or use a rotisserie**). Baste 3 times and turn chicken once so that it browns evenly. While chicken is roasting, gather and prepare the other ingredients.
3. Heat 1 qt. oil to 325 degrees and deep-fry peanuts for 5 minutes. Drain and cut into bits.
4. Deep-fry rice sticks for 3 minutes. (**They will increase in size about 4 times.**) Drain and set aside.
5. Toast sesame seeds by heating in dry frying pan over low heat until golden brown (**about 3 minutes**).
6. String the snow peas by removing the tips and the strings along the sides. Wash and cut into strips, julienne style.

*Flavored salt is, believe it or not, saltier than plain ol' salt. It will keep indefinitely if stored in a covered jar. To make it — Heat 2 T. salt in a dry frying pan over medium heat for 3 minutes. Remove from heat, add 1/8 t. five spice powder, and mix thoroughly. You may make as much as you desire, keeping the above proportions.

Continued

7. Cut celery into 2" pieces; then, cut each piece lengthwise into strips, julienne style.

8. Heat wok, add 1 T. oil, and stir-fry the snow peas, celery, and green onion for 3 minutes, sprinkling lightly with salt and sugar. Do not over-cook. Remove and set aside.

9. After it is roasted and cooled, the chicken should be boned and shredded by hand. Save the pieces of crisp skin and cut into strips, julienne style.

10. Mix the mustard with 1 t. water, add this to the chicken and then add the other ingredients listed under "B". Mix well by tossing.

11. Add the sitr-fried vegetables, lettuce and skin to the chicken. Again, mix well.

12. **NOW, JUST BEFORE SERVING--ADD** the "crispies" **(peanuts, seeds, rice sticks).** Mix lightly, and serve.

Note: The "Crispies" may be prepared a day or so in advance, and will retain their freshness if kept in a closed container.

Rice sticks are called **PY MEI FUN** and come in a soft package so labeled.

You will find this to be a delicious salad; its flavor is heightened by the crispness of the Chinese style vegetables and the crispies! Its charm and appeal is in the natural taste of the ingredients, not smothered or overpowered by a heavy dressing. Try it! You'll like it!

Serving Suggestions: CHINESE CHICKEN SALAD is great for a party dish, as a light summer meal, or as part of a multi-course dinner, as it requires neither heat nor refrigeration at the last minute.

COLD CHICKEN WITH ASPARAGUS
(Doong Lee Sun Gai)

Serves 4

1	whole chicken breast (approx. ¾ lb.)	
½ t.	salt	
¾ lb.	asparagus	
1 T.	oil	

SEASONING

1 T. sesame oil
1 T. thin soy sauce
1 T. cider vinegar
1 T. sugar
¼ t. salt
dash of pepper

1. Sprinkle chicken with ½ t. salt and then steam for 20 minutes. Set aside and shred when cooled.
2. Cut off and discard the last 2" at the base end of the asparagus. Then, cut each spear diagonally into 2" lengths. Wash and drain.
3. Combine "seasoning" in a bowl.
4. Heat wok, add oil and stir-fry asparagus for 4 minutes over medium heat.
5. Add shredded chicken and seasoning, mix well, and cook for 1 minute.
6. Chill in refrigerator for 1 hour before serving.

Note: This chicken dish must be served cold. Topping of toasted sesame seeds, slivered or chopped almonds, or chopped peanuts may be added.

Serving Suggestion: Serve with **TWICE COOKED PORK, NORTHERN STYLE VEGETABLE COVERED WITH EGG,** and **STEAMED RICE.**

Variation: Substitute sliced cucumber in place of asparagus.

CRISPY CHICKEN
(Chui Pei Gai)

Serves 8

3 lbs.	chicken
9 C.	water
1 T.	salt
1 T.	dark soy sauce
4	star anise
2	green onions, whole
½ t.	salt
2 T.	flavored salt*

COATING INGREDIENTS

¼ C.	boiling water
2 T.	vinegar
1½ T.	honey
2 T.	cornstarch

- - - - - - - - - - - - - - - - - -

1½ qts. oil for deep-frying

1. Rinse and clean chicken thoroughly.
2. In a large pot put 9 C. water, 1 T. salt, soy sauce, anise and green onions. Bring it to boil, covered, and cook for 20 minutes over medium heat.
3. Add chicken and cook for 8 minutes, **uncovered.**   Continually baste the chicken with the liquid in the pot.
4. Remove and dry the chicken with a paper towel.
5. Combine coating ingredients in a bowl. Use a pastry brush to coat outside of chicken. Let stand for 10 minutes. Repeat this procedure until 5 coats have been applied.
6. Tie a string around the chicken so that it can be hung in the air for 10 hours. **THEN:**
7. Heat oil to 350 degrees. Deep-fry chicken for 7 minutes on each side. Baste it with the oil as it is deep-frying.
8. Remove chicken, drain, and sprinkle inside and outside of chicken with ½ t. salt.
9. Chop chicken into 2" pieces and serve with "flavored salt" as a condiment.

*Flavored salt is saltier than plain salt and keeps indefinitely if stored in a covered jar. Heat 2 T. salt in a dry frying pan over medium heat for 3 minutes. Remove from heat, add 1/8 t. five-spice powder, and mix thoroughly. Make as much as you wish by following these proportions.

CURRIED CHICKEN WITH POTATOES
(Gah-Li Gai)

Serves 4

4 chicken thighs
  (approx. 1 lb. 2 ozs.)
2 medium-size red potatoes
½ yellow onion, large
2 T. oil
1 clove garlic, crushed
1 green onion, chopped
1 t. salt

1 t. sugar
1 T. white wine
1 T. oyster sauce
1½ T. curry powder
2 C. water
1 T. cornstarch
2 T. cold water

1. Chop each thigh into 5 pieces with the cleaver. Rinse carefully.
2. Peel and cut potatoes into 1" cubes.
3. Peel and cut yellow onion into 5 wedges.
4. Heat wok, add oil, garlic and chicken. Stir-fry the chicken for 5 minutes; then add potatoes.
5. Add all the remaining ingredients, **EXCEPT** the yellow onion, cornstarch and 2 T. water.
6. Bring to a boil, cover and cook for 20 minutes, over medium heat.
7. Add the yellow onion.
8. Add thickening made by combining the cornstarch and cold water. Cook for 1 minute, and serve.

Note: You may use already cut and packaged chicken. If pieces are large, serve American style...on a plate, and eat with a knife and fork.

Serving Suggestion: This recipe served over rice makes a good plate dinner.

DUCK AND POTATOES
(Sheu-Jai Mun Op)

Serves 8

1	fresh duck (4 - 5 lbs.)	2 T.	bean curd sauce (canned)
6	medium-size red potatoes	1½ t.	salt
20	small Chinese mushrooms	1 T.	sugar
2	green onions	1 T.	white wine
2 T.	oil	2 T.	thin soy sauce
2	cloves garlic, crushed	2 T.	oyster sauce
4 C.	chicken stock		dash of pepper
5	star anise*	2 T.	cornstarch
½ t.	five spice powder	4 T.	cold water

1. Clean and wash the duck. With the cleaver, chop the duck in half, then in quarters. Cut each quarter into 2" pieces.

2. Peel potatoes. Cut into 1½" cubes.

3. Soften Chinese mushrooms by soaking in water for ½ hour. Rinse, squeeze dry, cut off and discard stems.

4. Cut green onions into inch-long pieces.

5. Heat wok. When hot, add 1 T. oil and ½ of garlic. Then put in half of the duck pieces and braise to a nice color for 5 minutes. Set this aside.

6. Repeat step 5 using the remaining oil, garlic and duck.

7. In a large stewing pot, bring chicken stock to a boil. Add **ALL** remaining ingredients **EXCEPT** the red potatoes, cornstarch and 4 T. cold water. Again bring to boil; cover and cook over medium heat for ½ hour.

8. Now add the potatoes; cover and cook for 15 minutes more.

9. Add thickening made by combining the cornstarch and cold water. Cook for 1 minute, and serve.

*Sometimes the star anise are broken. There are supposed to be 5 points to each star.

Continued

Duck and Potatoes (Continued)

Note: This dish keeps well. You will find it equally good the next day.

Serving Suggestion: Serve this dish with **STEAMED RICE.**

Variations: I. Fresh chicken may be used instead of duck. If you use chicken, reduce the chicken stock to 2 cups and reduce the cooking time in step 7 from ½ hour to 15 minutes.

II. Beef stew meat may also be substituted for the duck. This should be cooked for the same amount of time as the duck.

FRIED CHICKEN, CANTONESE
(Jow Gai)

Serves 5

3 lbs.	chicken
1	green onion, chopped
1	thin slice ginger root chopped
3 T.	flour
4 T.	cornstarch
2 T.	water chestnut powder

- -

1 qt.	oil for deep-frying

MARINADE

1½ t.	salt
¾ t.	sugar
2 t.	thin soy sauce
1 t.	oyster sauce
1½ t.	white wine
¾ t.	five spice powder
	dash of pepper
1	egg white

1. Cut chicken into serving-size pieces.

2. Sprinkle chicken with each of the ingredients listed under "marinade", mix well and then add the green onion and ginger. Marinate for approximately 2 hours.

3. Combine flour, cornstarch and water chestnut powder in a bowl. Use this mixture to coat each piece of chicken just before dropping it into the hot oil.

4. Heat oil in wok to 350 degrees. Drop in the chicken and deep-fry for 15 minutes. Drain off excess oil, and serve.

FRIED SQUAB, CANTONESE
(Jow Bok Gop)

Serves 6

2	squabs (about 2¼ lbs. total)	
3	thin slices ginger, slivered	
1	green onion, slivered	
1	egg white	
3½ T.	water chestnut powder (in box)	
3½ T.	cornstarch	

- -

1 qt.   oil for deep-frying

MARINADE

1 t.	salt
1 t.	sugar
1½ t.	thin soy sauce
1 t.	oyster sauce
	dash of pepper
½ t.	five spice powder

1. Clean and wash squabs. Chop into 2" pieces.
2. Sprinkle squab with each of the ingredients listed under "marinade". Mix well and then add ginger, green onion and egg white. Marinate for 1 hour.
3. Mix water chestnut powder and cornstarch in a bowl. Use this mixture to coat each piece of squab just before dropping into the hot oil.
4. Heat oil to 325 degrees and deep-fry the squab for 15 minutes.
5. Remove from oil, drain on absorbent towels, and serve.

Note: Squab is a young pigeon, especially favored by the Chinese for its delicate texture and sweet taste. It is expensive and obtainable in Chinatown poultry shops.

Serving Suggestions: Serve fried squab on a bed of shredded lettuce, garnished with parsley.

Fresh lemon juice or flavored salt may be served with squab. For flavored salt recipe, see **CHINESE CHICKEN SALAD.**

GIZZARDS, CANTONESE
(See Yau Gai Sun)

Serves 6

1 lb.	gizzards (chicken)	2 C.	water
2	green onions	2 T.	sugar
2	star anise	½ t.	salt
½ t.	Szechuan type peppercorn*	1½ T.	thin soy sauce
½"	fresh ginger, crushed	1 T.	dark soy sauce
		1 T.	white wine

1. Thoroughly clean and rinse gizzards.

2. Cut green onions into 1" pieces.

3. Rinse star anise and peppercorn.

4. Put all ingredients, except gizzards, in a saucepan and bring them to a boil; then add the gizzards, cover and cook for 45 minutes over medium heat. **(Be sure to save about ¾ cup liquid.)**

5. Cut each gizzard lengthwise into 3 pieces, place in serving dish and pour the liquid over the gizzards.

Serving Suggestions: Serve either hot or cold. This makes a very tasty appetizer.

*Szechuan type peppercorn is **not hot** and has a very distinctive flavor. It can be purchased in a Chinese grocery store and isn't labelled. You have to ask for it. See **FOOD STUFFS USED IN CHINESE COOKING** for the Chinese name and characters.

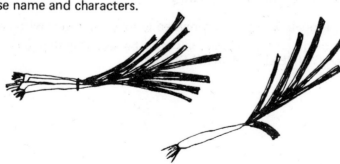

PAPER WRAPPED CHICKEN
(Gee-Bow Gai)

3½ lbs. chicken
45 sqs. unwaxed butcher paper
          or aluminum foil (6" x 6")
3   green onions, slivered
3   thin slices ginger, slivered

- -

2 qts. oil for deep-frying

MARINADE

2 t.   catsup
1 T.   oyster sauce
1½ t. hoisin sauce
1 t.   thin soy sauce
1 T.   white wine
        dash of pepper
1 t.   salt
1 t.   sugar
2 t.   cornstarch

1. Skin and bone chicken; then cut into pieces 1½" x 2" long.

2. Sprinkle chicken with each of the ingredients listed under "marinade", mix well and then add the green onions and ginger. Marinate for 2 hours.

3. See diagrams on next page for wrapping.

4. Heat the oil to 325 degrees and then carefully put each package into the oil. Deep-fry 4 minutes on each side. Put packages in a strainer to drain off excess oil before serving.

Note: **PAPER WRAPPED CHICKEN** may be deep-fried several hours in advance and reheated in the oven (325 degrees) for 10 minutes just before serving.

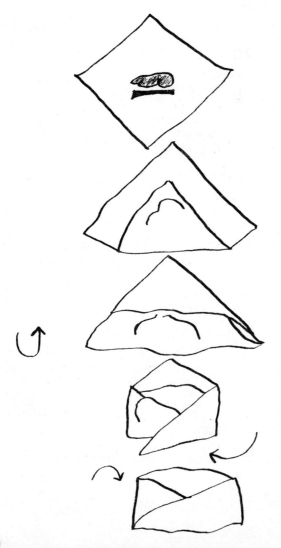

PAPER WRAPPED CHICKEN

1. Brush center of the paper with oil, and with one corner of the paper toward you, place 1 piece of chicken and 1 sliver of green onion about 2" from that corner.

2. Fold the corner to just cover the chicken.

3. Fold once more...about 1¼". (**This forms a triangle.**)

4. Make an envelope by folding the left and right corners toward the middle.

5. Tuck in the flap to close the envelope.

PINEAPPLE CHICKEN
(Bwo Luo Gai)

1 lb.	chicken parts
1	stalk celery
1	can chuck style pineapple (8 ozs.)
½ C.	water
½ T.	catsup
1 T.	vinegar
1¼ T.	sugar
	dash of salt
1 t.	cornstarch for thickening
2 t.	cold water for thickening

- -

2 C.	oil for deep-frying

MARINADE

½ t.	salt
½ t.	sugar
1 t.	thin soy sauce
	dash of pepper
1	thin slice ginger, chopped

BATTER

1	large egg
1 T.	water
2½ T.	flour
3 T.	cornstarch

1. Skin and bone chicken. Cut into 1½" cubes.

2. Sprinkle chicken with each of the ingredients listed under "marinade", mix well and marinate for ½ hour.

3. Cut celery into 1½" pieces; then, cut each piece lengthwise into strips, julienne style.

4. Drain pineapple, saving the juice.

5. Prepare batter by beating the egg, adding the water, flour and cornstarch. Mix thoroughly.

6. Heat oil to 350 degrees in a small saucepan.

7. Dip chicken in batter and drop into the hot oil. Deep-fry for 10 minutes. Remove and drain off excess oil.

8. In wok, combine pineapple juice, water, catsup, vinegar, sugar and dash of salt. Bring to a boil.

9. Add celery, chicken and pineapple. Cook for 1 minute over high heat.

10. Add thickening made by combining cornstarch and cold water. Cook for 1 minute and serve.

SOY SAUCE CHICKEN WINGS
(See Yau Gai Yick)

Serves 4

1 pkg.	chicken wings	½ C.	dark soy sauce
1½ C.	water	½ C.	thin soy sauce
5	star anise	1 T.	white wine
1	piece fresh ginger root (about ¾" thick), crushed	1 C.	brown sugar

1. Rinse and clean chicken wings thoroughly.

2. In a 2-quart saucepan bring water to a boil, add anise and boil for 10 minutes. There should be at least 1 C. of liquid remaining.

3. Add all remaining ingredients **EXCEPT** chicken wings and bring it to a fast boil.

4. Add chicken wings, cover and cook for 10 minutes more; turn off heat and let stand **(covered)** for 1 hour.

5. Remove chicken wings and serve. **(Be sure to save the sauce, putting it in the refrigerator for future use.)**

Note: The sauce can be used for 6 or 7 different preparations of chicken. Each time this dish is prepared there will be a little less sauce. Therefore, after 5 times you may need to add a little more of the various ingredients used in preparing the original sauce.

Serving Suggestions: This dish may be served hot or cold.
Serve with **RICE** and **CURRIED PRAWNS** or an egg dish.

Variations: I. Cook a whole chicken. Double the sauce recipe. Cook for 30 minutes, turn off heat and let stand in the covered pot for 1 hour. Chop in 2" x 1" x ½" pieces for easy eating. Put chopped chicken on a platter and pour a bit of the sauce over the chicken.

II. Use this sauce with spareribs. Cook the ribs for 30 minutes, turn off heat and let stand 1 hour.

III. Use 2 squabs and prepare the same way as given for spareribs.

STEAMED CHICKEN, CANTONESE
(Jing Gai)

Serves 6

2 lbs. chicken or chicken parts
10 small Chinese mushrooms
4 dried red dates (optional)
14 lily flower needles*
20 cloud ear (dried fungus)*
3 thin slices fresh ginger root, slivered
1 green onion, slivered

SEASONING

1¼ t. salt
1 t. sugar
1 t. thin soy sauce
1 t. dark soy sauce
1 t. oyster sauce
1 t. white wine
dash of pepper
1¾ T. cornstarch
1 t. cold water

1. Chop chicken into pieces about 1½" x ½".

2. Place chicken in a shallow dish or pie pan and add seasoning. Mix well.

3. Soak mushrooms, dried red dates, and lily flower needles in separate containers for 20 minutes. Rinse well. Squeeze moisture out of mushrooms and lily flowers.

4. Soak cloud ears for 15 minutes and **wash very thoroughly.**

5. Remove and discard stems of mushrooms and cut into thin strips, julienne style.

6. Remove seeds from red dates and cut the dates into thin strips.

7. Remove and discard ¼" off the hard end of each lily flower needle; then cut each needle in half.

8. Add mushrooms, red dates, lily flower needles, ginger and green onion to the chicken. Mix thoroughly, then steam for 20 minutes.

9. Add cloud ears and steam 10 minutes more.

Serving Suggestion: Serve with **RICE.** The juice is very tasty!

*These keep indefinitely and are found near the dried mushroom section in a Chinese grocery store.

EGG FOO YUNG
(Foo Yung Don)

½ lb.	fresh bean sprouts	½ t.	salt
½	yellow onion, med. size	½ t.	sugar
¼ lb.	Chinese barbecued pork	6	large eggs
10 T.	oil (approx.)	1 t.	oyster sauce
1	bamboo shoot tip (canned) or ½ C. sliced	½ t.	thin soy sauce
1	green onion, finely chopped		
1 T.	sesame seeds*		

1. Wash and drain bean sprouts.

2. Cut onion into thin slices.

3. Cut pork into thin strips, julienne style.

4. Heat wok, adding 1 T. oil. Stir-fry bean sprouts, onion, barbecued pork, and bamboo shoots for 2 minutes with ½ t. salt and ½ t. sugar (**Do not overcook.**) Let cool before using.

5. In a separate bowl beat the eggs, add oyster sauce and soy sauce; mix well.

6. Add the stir-fried ingredients and mix thoroughly.

7. Heat wok, add 1 T. oil and drop ½ C. of the mixture in the wok. Fry about 2 minutes on each side. Place on serving dish and set aside.

8. Repeat procedure with remaining oil and mixture.

9. Pour gravy, (See next page), over patties and garnish with the chopped green onion and toasted sesame seeds.

*Toast sesame seeds in a dry frying pan, without oil, for about 3 minutes.

Continued

EGG FOO YUNG GRAVY
(Foo Yung Don Hu Sui)

1	can OR	dash of pepper	
2 C.	clear chicken broth	1 t.	dark soy sauce
1/3 C.	sliced mushrooms (optional)	3 T.	cornstarch
½ t.	salt	6 T.	cold water
½ t.	sugar		

1. Bring broth to a boil.

2. Add mushrooms, salt, sugar, pepper and dark soy sauce.

3. Prepare thickening made with the cornstarch and cold water; add to the seasoned broth and cook for 1 minute.

Note: Without the gravy, the **EGG FOO YUNG** patties make great sandwich fillings!

EGGS WITH GREEN PEAS AND SHRIMP
(Chiang Dow Don)

Serves 4

¼ lb.	fresh shrimp
3	eggs
½ t.	dark soy sauce
	dash of salt
1 T.	oil
½ C.	frozen peas, defrosted
1	green onion, diced

SEASONING

1/8 t.	salt
1/8 t.	sugar
1/8 t.	thin soy sauce
	dash of pepper

1. Shell, devein, wash and dice shrimp.

2. Add "seasoning" and mix well.

3. Beat eggs, add dark soy sauce and dash of salt. Mix well.

4. Heat wok, add oil, and stir-fry shrimp, peas and green onion for 3 minutes over medium heat.

5. Pour the eggs over the shrimp mixture. Let cook for 1 minute. Turn with a spatula and scramble, as you do scrambled eggs, for 1 minute more.

Serving Suggestion: Serve with **SIZZLING RICE SOUP, BEAN SAUCE CHICKEN** and **STEAMED RICE.**

STEAMED EGGS, CANTONESE
(Jing Shui Don)

6	prawns (or ¼ C. cooked ham)	½ t.	salt
1/8 t.	thin soy sauce (for flavor)	¼ t.	oil
	dash of salt	1	green onion, finely chopped
2	eggs, large	1 t.	thin soy sauce*
1 C.	cold water		

1. Shell, devein, wash and cut prawns into very small bits. Add 1/8 t. thin soy sauce and a dash of salt. (**This flavoring step is omitted if ham is used, as it is sufficiently salty itself.**)

2. In a mixing bowl, beat the eggs, adding the water and the ½ t. salt.

3. Add the prawns (**or ham**) and mix well.

4. Heat water in your steaming utensil.

5. Oil a pie plate or similar dish (approximately 1½" deep) and place it on the steamer rack to heat for 1 minute.

6. Remove cover, pour egg mixture into the plate and cover.

7. Steam over medium heat for 10 minutes. (**Too high heat ruins the texture of the egg.**)

8. Sprinkle finely chopped green onion over the top of mixture; steam 1 minute longer.

9. Remove plate from steamer. Pour 1 t. soy sauce on top. Serve with rice.

Note: **STEAMED EGGS** appear similar to American custard, but are salty in taste rather than sweet. It is a simple dish to prepare and serve with rice for a satisfying lunch or dinner.

*For color when eggs are done.

STEAMED EGG CUSTARD
(Tiem Don Fah)

Serves 3

2 ozs.	Chinese rock sugar*
½ C.	water
3	medium size eggs

½ t.	almond extract
1½ t.	sweet shredded coconut (optional)

1. Dissolve the rock sugar in the water by boiling it for 5 minutes over medium-low heat. Let cool.
2. Beat the eggs, add sugar syrup and almond extract. Using a fork, mix well.
3. Pour mixture into custard cups that have been placed in a pie pan; then steam for 30 minutes. See **STEAMING HINTS.**
4. Uncover, sprinkle with coconut and steam for 3 minutes more.

Serving Suggestions: Serve either hot or cold.

*Chinese rock sugar is very similar to old fashioned rock sugar candy.

BEEF IN HOISIN SAUCE
(Hoisin Jerng Ngow Yuk)

Serves 4

½ lb.	flank or round steak
1½ T.	oil
1	clove garlic, crushed
2	green onions, slivered
1 t.	hoisin sauce
¼ t.	catsup
1 T.	chicken stock or water

SEASONING

½ t.	salt
1 t.	sugar
1 t.	thin soy sauce
½ t.	oyster sauce
	dash of pepper
1 T.	white wine
1 t.	cornstarch

1. Cut beef into 3 long strips (**cutting with the grain of the meat**). Cut each strip into thin slices, cutting across the grain.

2. Add "seasoning" to beef and mix well.

3. Heat wok, add oil and garlic, and stir-fry for 1 minute. Discard the garlic.

4. Add beef and green onion to the wok; stir-fry for 3 minutes.

5. Add hoisin sauce, catsup and chicken stock; mix thoroughly, cook for 2 minutes, and serve.

Serving Suggestions: Serve with **STEAMED RICE** or **NOODLES IN OYSTER SAUCE**. **BEAN SPROUTS WITH MIXED VEGETABLES** is a good complimenting dish.

BEEF IN OYSTER SAUCE
(Ho Yau Ngow Yuk)

Serves 4

1 lb.	flank steak
1	clove garlic, crushed
3	green onions, slivered
2 T.	oil
½ C.	chicken stock
2 T.	oyster sauce

MARINADE

1 t.	salt
½ t.	sugar
1 t.	thin soy sauce
2 t.	white wine
	dash of pepper
1 T.	cornstarch
3	thin slices fresh ginger, slivered

1. Cut flank steak into 3 long strips (with the grain of the meat). Cut each strip into thin slices, cutting across the grain.
2. Sprinkle meat with each of the ingredients listed under "marinade", mix well and marinate for 1 hour.
3. Heat wok, add oil and stir-fry garlic for 1 minute. Discard garlic if you wish.
4. Add marinated beef and stir-fry for 3 minutes.
5. Add green onions, chicken stock and oyster sauce. Bring to a boil, and serve.

Serving Suggestions: This dish can be served

  a. as one course of a multi-course dinner;
  b. over noodles for luncheon; or,
  c. as a plate dinner when served over steamed rice, having each serving garnished with a fried egg, sunny-side up.

BEEF STEW, CANTONESE
(Ngow Nom)

3½ lbs.	beef stew meat		2 T.	oil
2	green onions		1 t.	salt
1 T.	bean sauce (canned)		1½ t.	sugar
2	cloves garlic, crushed		1 T.	thin soy sauce
1	piece fresh ginger root, 1" thick		1 T.	white wine
				dash of pepper
1 T.	bean curd (canned)*		2 T.	oyster sauce
3	star anise (whole ones)		2½ T.	cornstarch
¼ t.	five spice powder		4 T.	cold water (for thickening)
1	chicken bouillon cube			
1½ qts.	water			

1. Remove fat from meat and cut into 1½" cubes.

2. Cut green onions into 1" lengths.

3. Rinse bean sauce one time and mash into a paste.

4. Heat wok, add 1 T. oil, ½ of the garlic and ½ of the meat. Stir-fry for 5 minutes. Remove from wok and repeat this procedure, using the remaining oil, garlic, and meat.

5. Put meat in a large pot and add all remaining ingredients except oyster sauce, cornstarch and the 4 T. of water. Mix well and bring to a boil. Cover and cook over medium heat for 1½ hours.

6. Add oyster sauce and thickening made by combining cornstarch and cold water. Stir in and bring to a boil, and serve.

Note: This stew will taste better on the second day.

Serving Suggestions: Serve over **STEAMED RICE** or on top of either **NOODLE SOUP** or **WON TON SOUP**.

*Canned bean curd will keep indefinitely in a closed container if stored in the refrigerator.

BEEF WITH FUZZY SQUASH
(Mo Gwah Ngow Yuk)

Serves 4

1/3 lb. flank steak
2 thin slices ginger, slivered
1 green onion, slivered
2 fuzzy squash*
3 T. oil
1 clove garlic, crushed
1 C. chicken stock or water
1½ t. cornstarch
3 t. cold water

SEASONING

1 t. salt
¼ t. sugar
1 T. thin soy sauce
1 t. oyster sauce
1½ t. cornstarch

1. Cut flank steak into 3 long strips (**cutting with the grain of the meat**). Cut each strip into thin slices, cutting across the grain.

2. Add ginger, green onion and "seasoning" to meat and mix well.

3. Peel squash and cut lengthwise into quarters; then, cut each quarter into slices ¼" thick.

4. Heat wok, add 2 T. oil and garlic. Stir-fry for 1 minute; then add beef and stir-fry for 3 minutes. Remove and set aside.

5. Heat wok, add 1 T. oil and squash. Stir-fry for 2 minutes; then add chicken stock (**or water**). Cover and cook for 8 minutes. (**If water is used, add salt to taste.**)

6. Uncover, add meat and mix well.

7. Thicken with a mixture made with the 1½ t. cornstarch and the 3 t. cold water. Cook for 1 minute, and serve.

Serving Suggestions: Serve over rice or serve as a dish to accompany **EGG FOO YUNG**.

*Fuzzy squash is slightly different from our squash. It is light green, about 5" long and 3" in diameter. Choose small sizes for tenderness.

CURRIED TRIPE
(Ga-Li Ngow Tu)

10 ozs.	tripe (beef)	½ t.	salt
1	stalk celery	1 t.	sugar
1	tomato	1 t.	thin soy sauce
1½ T.	oil	½ t.	oyster sauce
½"	piece fresh ginger root, crushed	1 T.	white wine
1	green onion, chopped		dash of pepper
1¼ T.	curry powder	1 t.	cornstarch
¾ C.	chicken stock	2 t.	cold water

1. Cut tripe into 1½" x 1" strips.
2. Parboil tripe for 2 minutes; drain.
3. Cut celery into 1½" pieces; then, cut each piece lengthwise into strips, julienne style.
4. Cut tomato in half; then, slice each half into four pieces.
5. Heat wok, add oil, ginger and green onion. Stir-fry for 1 minute.
6. Add tripe and stir-fry for 3 minutes.
7. Add curry powder, chicken stock, salt, sugar, thin soy sauce, oyster sauce, white wine and pepper. Cover and cook for 15 minutes.
8. Add celery and tomato. Bring to a boil.
9. Prepare thickening by combining cornstarch and cold water. Stir in, cook for 1 minute, and serve.

Serving Suggestion: Serve with **CRISPY CHICKEN, SPICE SHRIMP,** and **STEAMED RICE.**

GROUND BEEF AND NAPA CABBAGE
(Ngow Yuk Siu Choy)

Serves 4

1 lb. Napa cabbage
½ lb. ground beef
2 T. oil
½ t. salt
½ t. sugar

SEASONING

½ t. salt
½ t. sugar
    dash of pepper
2 t. white wine
1 t. thin soy sauce
2 t. cornstarch
2 t. water

1. Rinse, drain and cut cabbage into 1½" x ½" strips.
2. Add "seasoning" to the ground beef and mix well.
3. Heat wok, add 1 T. oil and the ground beef, separating the meat as you stir-fry it for 3 minutes. Then, set it aside.
4. Heat wok, add 1 T. oil and cabbage. Stir-fry for 3 minutes, adding ½ t. salt and ½ t. sugar.
5. Add ground beef, mix thoroughly and cook for 1 minute, and serve.

Serving Suggestion: Serve with **ORIENTAL PAN FRIED PRAWNS, SQUID WITH SNOW PEAS,** and **STEAMED RICE.**

84

TOMATO BEEF
(Fon Kehr Ngow Yuk)

1 lb.	flank steak
3	stalks celery
2	bell peppers
2	tomatoes
2 T.	oil
1	clove garlic, crushed
3/4 C.	chicken stock
3/4 T.	apple cider vinegar
4 t.	sugar
½ t.	salt
1 T.	catsup
1 T.	cornstarch
2 T.	cold water

SEASONING

1 t.	salt
½ t.	sugar
1 t.	thin soy sauce
1½ t.	oyster sauce
	dash of pepper
1 T.	cornstarch
1	green onion, slivered

1. Cut flank steak into 3 long strips (**cutting with the grain of the meat**). Cut each strip into thin slices, cutting across the grain.

2. Add "seasoning" to beef and mix well.

3. Cut celery into 1½" pieces; then, cut each piece lengthwise into strips, julienne style.

4. Remove seeds from bell pepper and cut into 1½" pieces.

5. Cut each tomato into eighths.

6. Heat wok and add 1 T. oil. Stir-fry celery and bell pepper for 3 minutes. Sprinkle lightly with salt and sugar. Remove and set aside.

7. Heat wok, add 1 T. oil, garlic and beef. Stir-fry for 3 minutes; remove and set aside with vegetables.

8. Put chicken stock in wok, add vinegar, sugar, salt and catsup. Bring to a boil.

9. Add tomatoes, vegetables and beef. Turn to high heat and bring to a boil again.

10. Prepare thickening using cornstarch and cold water. Stir into the mixture, cook for 1 minute, and serve.

CHINESE BARBECUED PORK
(Cha Siu)

Serves 5

1 lb.	lean pork butt
3/4 t.	salt
	dash of pepper
1 T.	sugar
1½ t.	thin soy sauce

1 t.	roasting salt*
1 t.	oyster sauce
½ t.	hoisin sauce
1 t.	white wine
1 T.	honey
¼ C.	water

1. Cut meat into pieces approximately 5" x 2" x 1".

2. Sprinkle meat with each of the remaining ingredients, except water, mix well, and marinate overnight **(or for at least 5 hours)** in the refrigerator.

3. Pre-heat oven at 375 degrees.

4. Put ¼ C. water in the roaster. Add pork and roast the meat for ½ hour on each side, basting 3 or 4 times.

Serving Suggestions: Serve as an hors d'oeuvre, sandwich filling, or over **WON TON SOUP** and **BASIC NOODLE SOUP,** as well as in **FRIED RICE, EGG ROLLS, SPICED NOODLES,** etc.

Note: Barbecued pork can be frozen for 3 months or refrigerated for 1 week.

*In this recipe you **must** use roasting salt for both the flavor and the red color. It may be purchased in a Chinese grocery store. See **FOOD STUFFS USED IN CHINESE COOKING** for the Chinese name and characters.

HAM WITH BEAN THREADS
(Huo Tui Fun See)

Serves 4

3 ozs. bean threads (packaged)
¼ lb. cooked ham. (approx ¾ C.)
1½ t. oil
2 C. chicken stock
1 green onion, slivered

½ t. salt
½ t. sugar
1 t. thin soy sauce
½ t. dark soy sauce

1. Soak bean threads in 1 quart of warm water for 1 hour and drain.
2. Cut ham into thin strips, julienne style.
3. Heat wok, add oil and stir-fry ham and bean threads for 1 minute.
4. Add chicken stock, salt, sugar and both soy sauces. Cook for 15 minutes over medium heat. (**The liquid will all be absorbed.**)
5. Add slivered green onion, and serve.

Serving Suggestions: Serve with **BOILED CHICKEN** and **WATERCRESS SOUP** or **EGG FLOWER SOUP.**

Variations: Chinese barbecued pork or chicken may be substituted for ham.

HOISIN SAUCE SPARERIBS
(Hoisin Jerng Pai Gwut)

Serves 6

2 lbs.	spareribs	1 T.	hoisin sauce (canned)
2 T.	oil	1 t.	catsup
1	clove garlic, crushed	1 T.	dark soy sauce
2	green onions, diced	1 t.	oyster sauce
1 t.	salt	1½ T.	white wine
1 t.	sugar	2 C.	water
1 t.	chili paste with garlic*	2 t.	cornstarch
		4 t.	water (for thickening)

1. Have the **butcher** cut the spareribs into pieces 1½'' wide and **you** cut the rib bones apart and trim off the fat.

2. Bring 2 quarts of water to a boil, and parboil the meat for 3 minutes; drain well.

3. Heat wok, add oil, garlic and green onion. Stir-fry for 1 minute.

4. Add spareribs and stir-fry for 5 minutes.

5. Add all remaining ingredients **except** cornstarch and the 4 t. water. Mix thoroughly, cover and bring to a boil. Reduce heat to medium and cook for 40 minutes.

6. Prepare thickening by combining the cornstarch with 4 t. cold water, and add to the sparerib mixture. Cook for 1 minute, and serve.

Note: "Chili Paste with Garlic" is quite spicy. Omit this seasoning if you don't care for "spicy" food.

Serving Suggestion: Serve with **LOTUS SOUP, CASHEW NUT SHRIMP,** and **STEAMED RICE.**

*Comes in a jar. Use Lan Chi Enterprises Co. Ltd. brand. Available in a Chinese grocery store.

PIGS FEET IN VINEGAR SAUCE
(Sheun Gee Gurk)

Serves 8

5 lbs.	fresh pigs feet	2	bottles Chinese black vinegar
2 qts.	water		(24 ozs.)*
1 t.	salt	½ C.	apple cider vinegar
¾ lb.	fresh ginger root	1 lb.	Chinese sugar bars*
		8	hard boiled eggs, shelled

1. Have butcher chop each foot into 6 equal pieces.

2. Bring 2 qts. water to a boil; add pigs feet and parboil for 7 minutes. Rinse and drain. Use small knife to scrape pieces clean; then sprinkle with salt.

3. Peel and cut ginger into thin slices.

4. **In an enamel pot** bring both kinds of vinegar to a boil. Add sugar and bring it to a boil again.

5. Add ginger, boiled eggs and pigs feet. Cover and cook for 1 hour, stirring occasionally. Taste sauce and add salt to taste.

6. Serve in individual bowls containing a small amount of the sauce.

Note: Pigs feet are a good source of protein. It has been the belief for many hundreds of years that mothers, after giving birth, regain strength and vigor by eating this dish. Friends or relatives, when the time of birth drew near, would gather at the mother-to-be's house. There they would all take part in scraping, cleaning, and preparing pigs feet. Naturally, after it was all ready, they would partake of it along with the new mother. In time, it became a tradition, and visitors of the new baby would always be welcomed with a bowl of pigs feet in vinegar. Today, if someone says, "Invite me over for pigs feet soon," it is his polite way of saying, "I hope you have a family soon."

This dish will keep for 2 weeks in the refrigerator; heat for 10 minutes before serving.

*Can be purchased in a Chinese grocery store.

PORK AND CHINESE SAUSAGE CAKES, STEAMED
(Gee Yuk Behng)

1	Chinese sausage*	1 t.	salt
4	fresh water chestnuts	½ t.	sugar
	(or 6 canned)**	1 t.	thin soy sauce
½ lb.	ground pork	¾ t.	oyster sauce
1	green onion, chopped	1 T.	cornstarch

1. Cut Chinese sausage into fine pieces; do the same with the water chestnuts.
2. In a shallow dish combine the ground pork, chopped water chestnuts, sausage and green onion.
3. Add all other ingredients and mix thoroughly.
4. Flatten and shape into a patty about 1" thick.
5. Using a wok or steampot, steam the meat for 25 minutes.

Note: This pork cake **must** be served over rice because it is too salty to eat alone. The juice tastes delicious with the rice.

*Chinese sausage can be kept in the refrigerator for 1 month.

If canned water chestnuts are used, stir-fry them in 1 t. oil for 1-2 minutes, adding 1 t. sugar; **cool before using.

PORK SPARERIBS WITH BLACK BEAN SAUCE

(See Jup Pai Gwut)

Serves 6

2 lbs.	pork spareribs	½ t.	salt
2 qts.	water	1 t.	sugar
2 T.	black beans	1 T.	thin soy sauce
2 T.	oil	1 T.	oyster sauce
1	clove garlic, crushed	2 T.	cornstarch
1	green onion, chopped	4 T.	cold water
2½ C.	chicken stock		

1. Have the **butcher** cut the spareribs into strips 1½" wide and **you** cut the rib bones apart and trim off the fat.

2. Bring 2 quarts of water to a boil, and parboil the meat for 3 minutes; drain well.

3. Wash black beans thoroughly two times; drain, and then crush beans with the handle of your cleaver or chop very fine with a sharp knife.

4. Heat wok, add oil, garlic and spareribs. Stir-fry for 5 minutes.

5. Add black bean mixture and all remaining ingredients **except** the cornstarch and 4 T. cold water. Bring to a fast boil and then turn to medium heat, cover, and cook for 40 minutes.

6. Make thickening with cornstarch and 4 T. cold water and add to the sparerib mixture. Bring to a boil again, and serve.

Note: **PORK SPARERIBS WITH BLACK BEAN SAUCE** will still taste delicious the second or third day. Reheat for 7 minutes before serving.

Serving Suggestion: Serve this dish over rice as a plate dinner, accompanied by a condiment prepared with either Chinese Hot Mustard or Coleman's Dry Mustard. Both require 2 t. dry mustard to 2 t. cold water.

Variations: I. Substitute raw chicken for the spareribs, eliminating parboiling, reducing the chicken stock to 1½ C. and cooking for 20 minutes.

Continued

91

Pork Spareribs with Black Black Bean Sauce (Continued)

Variations: II.   Substitute raw prawns, eliminating parboiling, reducing chicken stock to 1 C. and cooking for 5 minutes.

III.   Add 1 medium-size bell pepper to the recipe. Cut pepper into 1" pieces. Stir-fry for
3 minutes and add just before thickening.

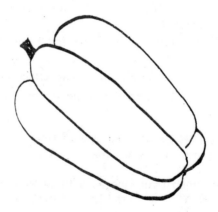

PORK WITH PICKLED MUSTARD
(Jah Choy Gee Yuk)

Serves 4

20   snow peas
¼ lb.   lean pork butt
4 ozs. pickled mustard (½ C.)*
¼   yellow onion
2 T.   oil
¼ C.   water

SEASONING

¼ t.   salt
¼ t.   sugar
1 t.   thin soy sauce
1 t.   cornstarch

1. Snap off the stem ends of the snow peas.

2. Cut pork, pickled mustard, yellow onion and snow peas into strips, julienne style, and put in separate bowls.

3. Soak pickled mustard in warm water for 15 minutes, rinse, and drain well.

4. Combine "seasoning" with pork strips.

5. Heat wok, add 1 T. oil, and stir-fry snow peas and yellow onion for 1 minute. Sprinkle lightly with salt and sugar and set aside.

6. Heat wok, add 1 T. oil, and stir-fry pork and pickled mustard for 3 minutes. Then add ¼ C. water, cover and cook for 4 minutes.

7. Add yellow onion and snow peas, mix well, and serve.

Serving Suggestion: Serve with **STEAMED RICE, HOT AND SOUR SOUP,** and **ABALONE WITH BOK CHOY.**

*Pickled mustard is quite salty and spicy. It can be kept in the refrigerator for 1 year.

PORK WITH STRING BEANS
(Dow Gawk Gee Yuk)

½ lb.	lean pork butt
1 lb.	string beans
1 T.	bean sauce (canned)
1	clove garlic, crushed
2 T.	oil
¼ C.	water
½ C.	chicken stock
¼ t.	salt
¼ t.	sugar
1 t.	cornstarch
2 t.	cold water

SEASONING

½ t.	salt
½ t.	sugar
1 t.	thin soy sauce
	dash of pepper
1	green onion, slivered
1 t.	cornstarch

1. Cut pork into thin strips, add "seasoning", and mix well.

2. Remove the ends of each string bean and cut diagonally into 3 pieces. Then parboil, uncovered, for 5 minutes.

3. Rinse bean sauce one time and mash into a paste; then add the crushed garlic.

4. Heat wok, add 1 T. oil and stir-fry pork for 3 minutes. Then add ¼ C. water, cover, and cook for 3 minutes more. Remove and set aside.

5. Heat wok, add 1 T. oil, and bean sauce mixture. Stir-fry for 1 minute.

6. Add string beans and stir-fry for 2 minutes. Then add salt, sugar, and ½ C. chicken stock. Cover and cook for 3 minutes.

7. Add pork and thickening mixture made by combining the cornstarch and 2 t. cold water. Cook for 1 minute; and serve.

STEAMED PORK WITH CHINESE RADISH
(Choy Po Jing Gee Yuk)

20	pieces Chinese radish (preserved)*	¾ t.	salt
1 t.	sugar	½ t.	sugar
½ lb.	lean pork butt	1 t.	thin soy sauce
2	thin slices fresh ginger root, slivered	¾ t.	oyster sauce
		1 t.	white wine
1	green onion, slivered	1 T.	cornstarch
1 t.	sugar	1 t.	water

1. Soak radish in warm water for 10 minutes. Then rinse, cut into ½" pieces, and sprinkle with the 1 t. sugar. Set aside.
2. Cut pork into thin slices. Put in a shallow dish.
3. Add remaining ingredients, except the radish, and mix thoroughly.
4. Steam for 15 minutes; then add radish and steam for 5 minutes more.

Note: Remaining radish will keep several months in a bag at room temperature.

Serving Suggestion: HOT PEPPER TOSS, CHICKEN MEAT BALL SOUP, STEAMED SALMON and STEAMED RICE are good accompanying dishes for a typical Chinese dinner.

*Preserved, salted radish, which come in a package, can be purchased in a Chinese grocery store.

SWEET AND SOUR PORK
(Tim-Sheun Yuk)

1 lb.	pork butt (pork spareribs may be used)
3	stalks celery
½	yellow onion
1	bell pepper
1	small can pineapple, chunk style (4 ozs.)
½ C.	pineapple juice*

- -

8 T.	cornstarch (for coating meat)
1 T.	oil
2 T.	cornstarch (for thickening)
4 T.	water

- -

1 qt.	oil for deep-frying

SWEET & SOUR SAUCE

1 C.	water
¼ t.	salt
¾ C.	sugar
½ C.	apple cider vinegar
2½ T.	catsup
½ t.	thin soy sauce

MARINADE

1 t.	salt
¼ t.	sugar
1 t.	thin soy sauce
1	egg white
1	green onion, chopped

1. Cut pork into 1" chunks.

2. Sprinkle meat with each of the ingredients listed under "Marinade", mix well, and marinate for 1 hour.

3. Cut celery into 1½" pieces; then cut each piece lengthwise into strips, julienne style.

4. Cut onion into 5 wedges.

5. Remove seeds and cut the bell pepper into 1" chunks.

6. Coat marinated pork with the cornstarch.

7. Heat 1 quart of oil to 325 degrees and deep-fry pork for 10 minutes. Drain on paper toweling.

8. Heat wok, add 1 T. oil and stir-fry the onion, celery and bell pepper for 2 minutes, adding a pinch of salt and a pinch of sugar. Remove from wok and set aside.

9. Using high heat, bring the ingredients listed under "Sweet and Sour Sauce" to a boil.

*Saved from the canned pineapple.

Continued

Sweet and Sour Pork (Continued)

10. Add celery mixture, cooked pork chunks, pineapple and the pineapple juice. Bring it to a boil again.

11. Add thickening made by mixing the 2 T. cornstarch with 4 T. cold water. Stir into the mixture, cook for 1 minute, and serve.

Note: Sweet and Sour Sauce can be made well in advance. It will keep 2 to 3 months if stored in a closed container in the refrigerator. **However,** don't add the pineapple juice and thickening mixture until ready to use.

TWICE COOKED PORK
(Hui Waw Yuk)

Serves 4

PART 1

1 lb.	lean pork butt
½	bell pepper
½	sweet red pepper
2	green onions, slivered
½"	piece fresh ginger root, crushed
1	star anise
1 t.	salt
1 t.	sugar
1 T.	white wine
3 C.	water

PART 2

1½ T.	bean sauce (Szechuan type)*
2 t.	sugar
1 t.	thin soy sauce
1 t.	sesame oil
2 T.	oil
2	cloves garlic, chopped
¼ C.	water
1 t.	cornstarch
2 t.	water (for thickening)

1. Combine ginger, anise, salt, sugar, white wine and water listed under Part 1. Bring it to a boil.

2. Add pork, cover and cook for 35 minutes over medium heat. Remove meat and cool. Discard the liquid.

3. Cut pork into strips about 1¼" x ½" x ¼".

4. Cut bell pepper and sweet pepper into 1¼" x ½" strips.

5. Mash bean sauce into a paste, put in a bowl and then add sugar, thin soy sauce and sesame oil.

6. Heat wok, add 1 t. oil, and stir-fry the pepper strips for 2 minutes, sprinkling lightly with salt. Set aside.

7. Heat wok, add remaining oil, garlic and pork; stir-fry for 2 minutes.

8. Add bean sauce mixture and continue stir-frying for 1 minute longer.

9. Add water and green onion. Cover and cook for 2 minutes.

10. Combine pepper strips with the meat mixture.

11. Make thickening by combining the cornstarch and cold water. Add to the meat mixture and cook for 1 minute more.

*Szechuan type bean sauce is spicy and very different from Cantonese bean sauce.

ABALONE IN OYSTER SAUCE
(Ho Yau Bau Yeu)

1 can abalone*
2 green onions, slivered

SAUCE

½ t. sugar
½ t. thin soy sauce
¾ t. sesame oil
1 T. oyster sauce
1 T. cornstarch
1 T. water

1. Remove abalone from can and save the liquid. Cut the abalone into very thin slices across the grain.
2. Bring abalone liquid to a boil.
3. Prepare sauce and add to boiling abalone liquid. Cook for 1 minute.
4. Add abalone and green onion. Heat only long enough to warm abalone (about 1 minute). Be sure not to overcook abalone or it will become very tough.

Serving Suggestion: Serve with **STEAMED RICE** and **LOTUS ROOT WITH PORK**.

*Be sure to buy expensive abalone as the cheaper brands are tough.

ABALONE WITH BOK CHOY
(Bau Yeu Bok Choy)

Serves 4

1 lb.	Bok Choy*	1 T.	oyster sauce
1	can abalone**	½ t.	sugar
2	green onions, slivered		dash of pepper
1 T.	oil	1½ t.	cornstarch
½ t.	salt	3 t.	cold water
½ t.	sugar		
¼ C.	chicken stock		

1. Break branches off center stock of bok choy, removing and discarding any flowers.

2. Peel outer covering off center stock; then cut diagonally into 2" pieces.

3. Cut off and discard about ¼" from the stem end of each leaf where it was attached to the center stock. Then, cut stems and leaves into 2" pieces.

4. Remove the abalone, saving the liquid for gravy, and cut it into thin slices across the grain.

5. Heat wok, add oil and stir-fry bok choy for 3 minutes; then add ½ t. salt, ½ t. sugar and the chicken stock. Bring it to a boil. Remove and arrange on a serving plate.

6. In the wok combine abalone liquid, oyster sauce, ½ t. sugar, pepper, and green onion. Bring to a fast boil.

7. Add abalone and cook for 1 minute.

8. Make thickening with the 1½ t. cornstarch and 3 t. cold water. Add to the abalone and cook for 1 minute. Pour over bok choy, and serve.

*Bok choy becomes crunchy when put in a container of cold water and placed in the refrigerator for about 2 hours.

**Be sure to buy an expensive brand of abalone as the inexpensive brands will be very tough. Heat rather than cook the abalone as it gets tough very easily.

CASHEW NUT PRAWNS
(Yiu Gwoh Ha)

Serves 4

½ lb.	fresh prawns
½	can mini sweet corn*
2	stalks celery
2	green onions
2 ozs.	raw cashew nuts (½ C.)
2 C.	water
1 t.	salt
1 T.	oil

- -

1 C.	oil for deep-frying

THICKENING MIXTURE

2 T.	water
1 t.	thin soy sauce
½ t.	dark soy sauce
	dash of pepper
1½ t.	cornstarch

1. Shell, devein and wash prawns; then, put 1 t. salt into 2 C. water. Add the prawns and soak for 1 hour.

2. Cut each mini corn diagonally into 2 parts.

3. Cut celery into 1½'' pieces; then cut each piece lengthwise into strips, julienne style.

4. Cut green onions into ¾'' lengths.

5. Drain and dry prawns with a paper towel.

6. In a small saucepan heat 1 C. oil to 325 degrees. Then, deep-fry the cashew nuts for 3 minutes or until golden brown. Drain off excess oil and set aside.

7. Using the same oil as used for the cashew nuts, deep-fry the prawns for 3 minutes. Remove and set aside.

8. Heat wok, add 1 T. oil and stir-fry celery, sweet corn and green onion for 1 minute, sprinkling lightly with salt and sugar.

9. Add prawns.

10. Combine thickening ingredients in a cup; then stir into prawn mixture. Cook for 1 minute.

11. Turn off heat, add cashew nuts, mix thoroughly, and serve.

*Mini sweet corn may be purchased in a Chinese grocery store or in the gourmet section of your favorite grocery store. Unused corn will keep for one week in the refrigerator or can be used in place of celery or snow peas in preparing another dish.

CURRIED PRAWNS
(Ga-Li Ha)

Serves 4

6 ozs.   fresh prawns, medium size
½   yellow onion
1 T.   oil
1   green onion, chopped
1 T.   curry powder
1/3 C. chicken stock or water

SEASONING

¼ t. salt
¼ t. sugar
½ t. thin soy sauce
½ t. oyster sauce
      dash of pepper

1. Shell, devein, wash and drain prawns.
2. Add "seasoning" to prawns and mix well.
3. Cut yellow onion into 5 wedges.
4. Heat wok, add oil and stir-fry prawns, yellow onion and green onion for 2 minutes.
5. Add curry powder and chicken stock. Cook for 2 minutes, and serve.

Serving Suggestions: Serve over rice as a one dish meal, or serve with **OYSTER BEEF** as one of two dishes for dinner.

ORIENTAL PAN-FRIED PRAWNS
(Jeen Ha)

6 ozs. fresh prawns,* medium size
1   green onion, chopped
1½ T.   oil
4 T.   cold water
1 T.   oyster sauce

1 t.   sugar
1 T. & ½ t.   catsup
¼ t.   salt
              dash of pepper

1. Prepare the prawns by cutting off whiskers with scissors. Slit shell along the back and devein. Wash and drain well.

2. Combine the chopped green onion, water, oyster sauce, sugar, catsup, salt and pepper in a bowl.

3. Heat wok, add oil, and pan-fry the prawns for 2 - 3 minutes on each side.

4. When prawns are golden red, add the prepared mixture. Heat to a boil over high flame. (**It is not necessary to thicken this dish with cornstarch because the catsup and oyster sauce serve as thickening.**)

*Prawns may be shelled or unshelled. If shelled before cooking, the prawns will be less tender but easier to eat.

SHELLING AND DEVEINING A PRAWN
(Hee Ha Cherng)

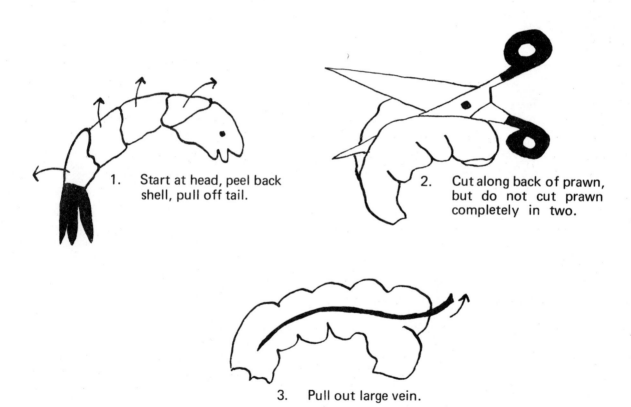

1. Start at head, peel back shell, pull off tail.

2. Cut along back of prawn, but do not cut prawn completely in two.

3. Pull out large vein.

SPICED SHRIMP
(Laht Ha)

Serves 4

½ lb. fresh prawns
2 cloves garlic, chopped
½ t. salt
½ t. sugar
    dash of pepper
1 T. oil

- - - - - - - - - - - - - - - - - - -

2 C. oil (for deep-frying)

BATTER

1 large egg
2 T. flour
1¼ T. cornstarch

SAUCE

2 T. thin soy sauce
1 T. cider vinegar
1 T. sesame oil
1¼ T. sugar
5 dried chili peppers, finely chopped

1. Shell, devein and wash prawns. Drain and pat dry with paper towels.

2. Add salt, sugar and pepper, mixing well.

3. While oil is heating to 350 degrees, prepare the batter by beating the egg, adding the flour and cornstarch. Mix thoroughly.

4. Dip prawns in batter, drop in hot oil and deep-fry for 4 minutes. Remove and drain off excess oil.

5. Prepare sauce by combining the listed ingredients.

6. Heat wok, add 1 T. oil, and stir-fry garlic for 1 minute. Add sauce and bring to a boil.

7. Add deep-fried prawns, mix thoroughly, and serve.

Note: A small saucepan can be used for deep-frying small amounts.

Serving Suggestions: This appetizer may be served hot or cold or as one of the dishes in a Chinese dinner, including **LETTUCE SOUP, PINEAPPLE CHICKEN,** and **STEAMED RICE.**

105

STEAMED PRAWNS WITH BLACK BEANS
(See Jup Jing Ha)

¾ lb.	raw prawns		½ t.	salt
1¼ T.	black beans		1 t.	sugar
1	clove garlic, chopped		1½ t.	thin soy sauce
1	green onion, chopped		1 t.	white wine
1 T.	oil		1 t.	oyster sauce

1. Prepare the prawns by cutting off whiskers, cutting along the top of the shell, and deveining them. Leave the shells on the prawns because this keeps the prawns more tender, tasty and plump. Wash, drain and put prawns in a pie pan so as to be ready for steaming.

2. Wash black beans two times and mash into a paste; then add the chopped garlic.

3. Combine remaining ingredients, **except** the oil.

4. Pour mixture over prawns; then, pour oil on top.

5. Cover and steam for 10 minutes.

Serving Suggestion: This dish must be served with steamed rice. The juice is very tasty.

STEAMED SALMON, CANTONESE
(Jing Sa-Mon Yeu)

Serves 4

1½ lbs.   fresh salmon
1   piece fresh ginger, approx.
        1" long and ¼" thick
1   green onion, slivered

SEASONING

1½ t.   salt
1 t   dark soy sauce
2 t.   thin soy sauce
1½ t.   white wine
1 t.   sugar
1 T.   oil
        dash of pepper

1. Clean and scale fish; then put in a shallow dish.
2. Peel and sliver ginger, julienne style.
3. Put ingredients listed under "seasoning" on top of fish.
4. Add green onion and ginger as topping.
5. Steam for 20 minutes, and serve.

Note: Other kinds of fish may be used, such as perch, rock cod or sand dab.

Serving Suggestion: This dish must be served with **STEAMED RICE.**

STEAMED SAND DAB

(Jing Top Sah Yeu)

2	sand dab	½ t.	salt
1 T.	bean sauce (canned)	½ t.	sugar
3	thin slices ginger, slivered	1 T.	thin soy sauce
1	green onion, chopped	1 t.	oyster sauce
			dash of pepper
		1 T.	oil

1. Remove fins and tails, rinse, and cut each fish into 3 equal parts.

2. Rinse bean sauce in a small amount of water, drain and mash into a paste.

3. Add salt, sugar, soy sauce, oyster sauce, pepper, bean sauce, ginger, green onion and oil to the fish in that order.

4. Steam for about 10 minutes.

Note: Other kinds of fish may be used, such as perch, rock cod or salmon. Fish steamed this way is very tasty. It is a natural accompaniment to steamed rice in a bowl, when eaten with chopsticks in the Chinese manner.

Serving Suggestion: Serve with **STEAMED RICE, CHINESE BOILED CHICKEN,** and a vegetable dish like **CHINESE STRINGBEANS WITH PRAWNS** for a typical family dinner.

STIR-FRIED CRAB
(Chow Hai)

Serves 3

1¼ lbs. live crab*
2 green onions
2 T. oil
1 clove garlic, crushed
1 piece ginger (½"), crushed

¼ t. salt
¼ t. sugar
1 t. thin soy sauce
2 t. white wine
dash of pepper
¼ C. water

1. See the following page for preparing crab for stir-frying.
2. Cut the green onions into 1½" pieces.
3. Heat wok, add oil, garlic, ginger and onions.
4. Add the crab and stir-fry for 3 minutes.
5. Add remaining ingredients, cover and simmer for 6 minutes.

Note: When crab is prepared this way, it has a deliciously different flavor from the usual "boiled crab".

Serving Suggestion: Serve with **EGG FLOWER SOUP, STEAMED RICE,** and **CANTONESE STEAMED CHICKEN.**

Variation: For another "taste treat", freshly killed crab can be chopped into pieces, sprinkled with slivered ginger, and steamed for 10 minutes.

*If the crab is purchased at a Chinese market, the clerk will kill the crab for you.

HOW TO PREPARE LIVE CRAB FOR COOKING:
(Ju Hai Fong Fat)

1. Insert chopstick into rear crevice of crab **(between the shell and the body).** Use chopstick as a lever, at the same time pull at the shell with your hand to remove it from the rest of the body.

2. Remove the finger-like projections, soft air sacs, by simply pulling them off. Cleanse under running water.

3. Chop crab into approximately six to eight equal pieces. When chopping crab, try to portion a piece of the body with each piece of claw.

4. For easy eating, use a hammer to crack the claws.

5. Now remove the "crab butter" from along the edges where it is attached to the shell. Add this to the crab when you stir-fry.

SQUID WITH SNOW PEAS
(Chow Yau Yeu)

Serves 4

1 lb. squid
¼ C. cloud ear (packaged)
25 snow peas
7 water chestnuts (fresh
    or canned)
½ can bamboo shoot tips*

2 T. oil
1 thin slice fresh ginger

¼ t. salt
¼ t. sugar
1 t. thin soy sauce
    dash of pepper
¼ C. chicken stock
1 t. cornstarch
2 t. water

1. Cut off each squid head above the eyes. Save the head. Slit the body lengthwise, remove cartilage and entrails, and scrape off the skin. Rinse and drain well.
2. Cross-score the inner side of each squid and cut into 3 pieces. This makes the squid curl into little rolls, which are appealing to the eye.
3. Soak the cloud ears for 10 minutes and clean thoroughly.
4. Remove tips from the snow peas; then cut diagonally into two pieces.
5. Peel the fresh water chestnuts. **(Canned ones are already peeled.)** Cut into thin slices.
6. Heat wok, add 1 T. oil and stir-fry bamboo shoots, snow peas, cloud ears and water chestnuts for 2 minutes, sprinkling lightly with salt and sugar. **(If canned water chestnuts are used, stir-fry them separately in 1 t. oil for 1 - 2 minutes, adding 1 t. sugar.)** Set aside.
7. Heat wok, add 1 T. oil and the ginger. Stir-fry for 1 minute.
8. Add squid and stir-fry for 3 minutes.
9. Add salt, sugar, thin soy sauce, dash of pepper and the ½ C. chicken stock. Bring it to a boil and cook for 2 minutes more.
10. Add bamboo shoot mixture. Mix thoroughly.

*Buy water pack bamboo shoot tips in 15 oz. can.

Continued

11. Make thickening using the cornstarch and 2 t. cold water. Add to the mixture and cook 1 minute longer, and serve.

Note: Squid prepared in the Chinese style is very tender and tasty.

For some inexplicable reason, the Chinese say one has "Chow Yau Yeu", when one is fired from one's job. This is a very polite way of communicating the distasteful fact that one has been discharged by his employer. For this reason, "Chow Yau Yeu" is **NEVER** served on auspicious occasions, such as New Year's Day.

Serving Suggestion: For a very satisfying dinner, serve this dish with **BEEF WITH FUZZY MELON, BLACK BEAN SPARERIBS,** and **STEAMED RICE.**

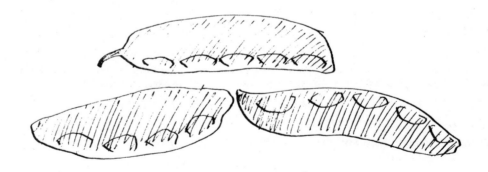

BEAN SPROUTS WITH MIXED VEGETABLES
(Chow Ngah Choy)

Serves 6

1 lb.	bean sprouts	½ t.	thin soy sauce
2	stalks celery	1 t.	dark soy sauce
1	sweet red pepper*	1 t.	sugar
2	green onions, slivered	1 t.	salt
1 T.	oil	½ C.	chicken stock
		1 T.	cornstarch
		2 T.	cold water

1. Wash bean sprouts in cold water and drain.

2. Cut celery into 1½" pieces, then cut each piece lengthwise into strips, julienne style.

3. Remove seeds from pepper, and cut into thin strips, julienne style.

4. Heat wok, add oil, and quickly add all vegetables; stir-fry for 3 minutes.

5. Add all remaining ingredients, **EXCEPT** cornstarch and 2 T. cold water. Mix thoroughly, let cook for 2 minutes, uncover.

6. Add thickening made by mixing the cornstarch with 2 T. cold water, cook for another ½ minute, and serve.

Serving Suggestion: Serve with **EGGS WITH GREEN PEAS AND SHRIMP, PINEAPPLE CHICKEN,** and **STEAMED RICE.**

*Green bell pepper may be substituted.

BROCCOLI WITH CHICKEN
(Gai Chow Guy Lon)

Serves 6

1¼ lbs. broccoli
1 lb. chicken parts
3 T. oil
½ t. salt
½ t. sugar
½ t. thin soy sauce
1/3 C. chicken stock
¼ C. water

SEASONING
½ t. salt
½ t. sugar
1 t. thin soy sauce
1 t. oyster sauce
1 t. white wine
dash of pepper
1 T. cornstarch
1 green onion, slivered
3 thin slices ginger root, slivered.

1. Peel off outer covering from broccoli stems. Cut into 1½" x ½" pieces.

2. Skin and bone chicken. Cut into 1½" x ½" pieces.

3. Add "seasoning" to chicken, and mix well.

4. Heat wok, add 1 T. oil, and stir-fry broccoli for 2 minutes.

5. Add salt, sugar, soy sauce and chicken stock. Bring it to a boil, uncovered, and cook for 4 minutes. Set aside in a bowl.

6. Heat wok, add 2 T. oil and stir-fry chicken for 3 minutes.

7. Add water, cover and cook for 4 minutes longer.

8. Add broccoli, mix thoroughly, and serve.

Note: When broccoli is cooked uncovered it keeps its bright green color. It also stays nice and crunchy.

Serving Suggestion: Serve with **EGG FLOWER SOUP, SWEET AND SOUR PORK,** and **STEAMED RICE.**

Variations: Beef, pork, or prawns may be substituted for the chicken.

CHINESE MUSHROOMS WITH BAMBOO SHOOTS
(Doong Goo Jook Sun)

Serves 4

25	Chinese mushrooms, small	½ t.	salt
2	stalks celery	½ t.	sugar
10	snow peas	1 t.	cornstarch
½	can bamboo shoot tips*	1 t.	dark soy sauce
1 T.	oil	3 t.	cold water

1. Boil mushrooms for 10 minutes, rinse and squeeze dry. Remove and discard stems.

2. Remove celery strings with a vegetable peeler and cut into 1½'' pieces; then cut each piece lengthwise into strips, julienne style.

3. Snap off the stem end of the snow peas, and cut into thin strips, julienne style.

4. Heat wok, add 1 T. oil, and stir-fry mushrooms, bamboo shoots, celery and snow peas for 3 minutes, adding salt and sugar.

5. Make thickening by combining cornstarch, dark soy sauce and water in a cup. Stir into the mixture and cook for 1 minute, and serve.

Serving Suggestion: Serve with any kind of meat dish, such as **BEEF IN OYSTER SAUCE, STEAMED PORK AND CHINESE SAUSAGE CAKES,** or **TWICE COOKED PORK.**

*Buy water pack bamboo shoot tips in 15 oz. can.

CHINESE STRING BEANS WITH PRAWNS
(Dow Gok Chow Ha Kau)

Serves 4

½ lb.	Chinese string beans*
½ lb.	raw prawns
¾ T.	bean sauce (canned)**
2 T.	oil
¼ t.	salt
½ t.	sugar
¾ C.	chicken stock
1 T.	cornstarch
2 T.	cold water

SEASONING

½ t.	salt
½ t.	sugar
1	green onion, chopped
1 t.	thin soy sauce
	dash of pepper

1. Snap off and discard ends of Chinese string beans; then cut beans into 2" lengths.
2. Shell, devein and wash prawns, add "seasoning", and mix well.
3. Rinse bean sauce in cold water one time and crush with the handle of the cleaver.
4. Heat wok, add 1 T. oil, and stir-fry prawns for 3 minutes and set aside.
5. Heat wok, add 1 T. oil, bean sauce and string beans and stir-fry for 3 minutes.
6. Add salt, sugar and chicken stock, cover and cook for 4 minutes.
7. Prepare thickening by combining cornstarch and cold water. Add to the dish, cook for 1 minute, and serve.

Serving Suggestion: Serve with **STEAMED EGGS** and a soup.

Variations: Beef or chicken may be substituted for prawns.

*Regular string beans may be substituted for the Chinese variety.

Bean sauce **must be rinsed; otherwise it is too salty.

CHOW BEAN CAKE
(Chow Dow Foo)

8	squares bean cake*		¼ t.	salt
¼ lb.	barbecued pork		1 t.	sugar
2 T.	bean sauce (canned)		½ t.	thin soy sauce
1	clove garlic, crushed		1½ t.	oyster sauce
2	green onions, slivered		1 C.	chicken stock
1 T.	oil		1½ t.	cornstarch
			3 t.	water

1. Cut each bean cake into 1'' cubes.
2. Cut pork into very thin slices.
3. Rinse bean sauce one time and mash into a paste; then add garlic.
4. Heat wok, add 1 T. oil, bean sauce mixture and bean cake; stir-fry 1 - 2 minutes.
5. Add salt, sugar, soy sauce, oyster sauce and chicken stock. Heat quickly, then cover and cook for 2 - 3 minutes over moderate heat.
6. Add pork and slivered green onions and bring to a boil.
7. Thicken with cornstarch which has been mixed with 3 t. cold water. Cook for 1 minute, and serve.

Serving Suggestions: CHOW BEAN CAKE makes a plate lunch when served over rice OR it can be served along with several other dishes for a Chinese dinner.

Variations: Ham, shrimp, or beef may be substituted for the barbecued pork.

*Buy **firm** kind of bean cake for cooking.

HOT PEPPER TOSS
(Laht Jiu Soong)

1	bell pepper, med. size		2 T.	oil, approx.
5	fresh chili peppers		3 T.	cold water
2	green onions		½ t.	salt
¼ lb.	Chinese barbecued pork		½ t.	sugar
8	water chestnuts, fresh or canned*		1/3 C.	chicken stock
2	stalks celery		1 t.	oyster sauce
30	dried shrimp		1 t.	cornstarch
1 T.	black beans (packaged)		2 t.	cold water (for thickening)

1. Cut peppers in half, remove seeds and dice.
2. Dice green onions, barbecued pork and water chestnuts. Combine in a bowl.
3. Dice celery and put in a separate bowl.
4. Soak dried shrimp in warm water for 5 minutes. Rinse and drain.
5. Rinse black beans two times and mash them into a paste.
6. Heat wok, add 1 t. oil, and stir-fry barbecued pork, green onions, and water chestnuts for 2 minutes. Set aside.
7. Heat wok, add 1 t. oil, and stir-fry dried shrimp for 1 minute. Then, add 3 T. water and simmer for 2 minutes. Set aside.
8. Heat wok, add 1 T. oil and stir-fry black bean paste for 1 minute. Then add both kinds of peppers and celery. Stir-fry for 2 minutes more, adding the salt and sugar.
9. Add chicken stock and cook for 2 minutes.
10. Add barbecued pork mixture and oyster sauce.
11. Make thickening by combining cornstarch and the 2 t. cold water. Add to the mixture and cook for 1 minute, and serve.

Note: **HOT PEPPER TOSS** is a typical home dish which blends beautifully with the bland taste of steamed rice.

*Fresh water chestnuts must be peeled. Canned ones should be stir-fried with 1 t. oil for 1 - 2 minutes, adding 1 t. sugar to bring out the flavor.

LOTUS ROOT WITH PORK
(Lin Ngau Chow Gee Yuk)

Serves 3

¼ lb. lean pork butt
20 pieces cloud ear (dried fungus)
20 snow peas
1 stalk celery
¼ lb. lotus root*
2 T. oil
½ C. water
1 t. sesame oil
½ t. dark soy sauce

SEASONING

¼ t. salt
¼ t. sugar
½ t. thin soy sauce
  dash of pepper
1 t. cornstarch

1. Cut pork into thin strips, 1" x ½".
2. Add "seasoning" to pork and mix well.
3. Soak cloud ears for 10 minutes; rinse thoroughly, and drain.
4. Remove tips from snow peas; cut diagonally into 2 parts.
5. Cut celery into 1½" pieces; then cut each piece lengthwise into strips, julienne style.
6. Peel and cut lotus root in thin slices and then cut each slice in half.
7. Heat wok, add 1 T. oil, and stir-fry snow peas, celery, and cloud ears for 2 minutes, sprinkling lightly with salt and sugar. Remove and set aside.
8. Heat wok, add 1 T. oil, and stir-fry pork for 2 minutes.
9. Add lotus root and water. Cover and cook for 4 minutes.
10. Add snow pea mixture, sesame oil, and dark soy sauce. Mix thoroughly, and serve.

*Lotus root must be purchased in a Chinese grocery store. It will stay fresh for 2 weeks in the refrigerator.

MUSHROOMS IN OYSTER SAUCE
(Ho Yau Doong Goo)

Serves 5

3 ozs.	Chinese mushrooms (about 45 of small size)
1	green onion AND
3	green onions (use bottoms only)
1 T.	oil
1 in.	piece ginger, crushed
1 T.	white wine

1 t.	sugar
3 C.	chicken stock
1 T.	oyster sauce
1 t.	dark soy sauce
1 T.	cornstarch
2 T.	cold water

1. Soften mushrooms by soaking in cold water for ½ hour. Rinse, squeeze dry, cut off and discard stems.

2. Cut one green onion into halves, to be used in cooking. The 3 green onion bottoms are to be cut into slivers and used as garnish.

3. Heat wok, add 1 T. oil and the mushrooms. Stir-fry for 3 minutes. Then add the green onion, ginger, wine, sugar and chicken stock.

4. Bring the mixture to a quick boil. Turn fire to medium-low heat. Cover and cook for 1 hour. Stir occasionally, being sure there is sufficient liquid remaining. There should be at least 1 cup of liquid remaining to make into a sauce.

5. After 1 hour, add the oyster sauce and the dark soy sauce.

6. Mix cornstarch with 2 T. cold water. Add this mixture to the mushrooms, and cook, stirring over high heat, for 1 minute.

7. Serve in platter, garnished with slivers of green onion.

Note: **CHINESE MUSHROOMS** make a very good "company" dish. The mushrooms are a delicacy, expensive, and becoming more and more difficult to purchase. This method of preparation accords to the mushroom the proper treatment it deserves!

Serving Suggestion: Serve with **HOISIN SAUCE SPARERIBS** and **TOMATO BEEF CHOW MEIN**.

NORTHERN VEGETABLES COVERED WITH EGG
(Wau Choy Dai Mo)

20	cloud ears (dried fungus)	½ t.	salt
10	lily flower (golden needles)	½ t.	sugar
2 ozs.	bean threads	1 t.	dark soy sauce
½ lb.	fresh spinach	¾ T.	sesame oil
¼ lb.	bean sprouts	1 C.	chicken stock
1	green onion, slivered	2	large eggs, beaten
2 T.	oil	4 t.	milk

1. Soak cloud ears for 10 minutes; then, wash thoroughly, and drain.

2. Soak lily flowers and bean threads for 20 minutes. Rinse and drain.

3. Cut ½" off pointed ends of lily flowers. Then cut each lily flower in half.

4. Clean spinach, cut off and discard ½" from stem end and break into 2" pieces.

5. Heat wok, add 1 T. oil and stir-fry cloud ears, spinach, bean sprouts and green onion for 3 minutes.

6. Add salt, sugar, dark soy sauce and sesame oil. Mix thoroughly, remove and set aside.

7. Put chicken stock, bean threads and lily flowers in wok. Bring it to a boil, cover and cook for 10 minutes over medium heat. All the liquid should be absorbed.

8. Add the cloud ear mixture and mix well. Put in serving dish.

9. Combine eggs and milk and beat as you would for scrambled eggs.

10. Heat 9" frying pan, add 1 T. oil and pan fry the egg mixture, covered and without stirring, for 1 minute.

11. Cover the vegetables with the egg patty, and serve.

Note: Steps 8 - 10 must be timed so that the vegetables don't get cold.

SPICED CABBAGE
(Lot Yeh Choy)

Serves 6

1 lb.	cabbage		2 t.	sugar
1 T.	sesame oil		¼ t.	salt
1 T.	thin soy sauce		1 T.	oil
1 T.	cider vinegar		½ t.	chili paste with garlic (in jar)*

1. Cut cabbage into pieces approximately 1½" x ½".

2. Combine sesame oil, thin soy sauce, vinegar, sugar and salt in a bowl.

3. Heat wok, add oil and stir-fry cabbage for 3 minutes.

4. Add chili paste and sesame oil mixture. Mix well.

5. Chill in the refrigerator for 2 hours before serving.

Serving Suggestion: Serve with **CANTONESE BEEF STEW, ORIENTAL PAN FRIED PRAWNS,** and **STEAMED RICE** for a very satisfying dinner.

*Omit chili paste if you don't enjoy spicy food.

SPICED EGGPLANT
(Lot Ker Jee)

Serves 3

6 ozs.	Oriental eggplant	¼ t.	salt
1	green onion, chopped	¼ t.	sugar
1	clove garlic, finely chopped	4 T.	chicken stock
1	thin slice ginger, chopped	¾ t.	thin soy sauce
1 t.	chili paste with garlic*	¾ t.	apple cider vinegar
5 T.	oil	¾ t.	sesame oil

1. Cut eggplant into slices ¼" thick and on the diagonal.

2. Heat wok, add 4 T. oil and pan-fry eggplant approximately 1½ minutes on each side. Remove and drain off excess oil on paper towels.

3. Heat wok, add 1 T. oil, garlic, ginger and chili paste. Stir-fry for 1 minute. Then, add salt, sugar, soy sauce, chicken stock and eggplant. Bring it to a boil.

4. Add vinegar, sesame oil and green onion. Remove from heat, and serve.

Serving Suggestion: Serve with **HOT AND SOUR SOUP, CRISPY CHICKEN,** and **STEAMED RICE.**

*Can be purchased in a Chinese grocery store. The "chili paste with garlic" is made by the Lan Chi Co. in Taiwan. It comes in a jar. Omit the chili paste if you don't enjoy spicy foods.

SPINACH WITH BEAN CAKE PASTE
(Fu Yeuh Bwo Choy)

1 lb. spinach	½ C. chicken stock
1½ T. oil	½ t. salt
1 clove garlic, crushed	½ t. sugar
¾ T. bean cake paste (in jars)	

1. Wash spinach thoroughly. Cut off and discard ½" of the stems. Cut spinach leaves in halves for easier eating.

2. Heat wok and add oil, garlic and bean cake paste. Stir-fry for 1 minute, add spinach, and stir-fry for approximately 4 minutes more.

3. Add the chicken stock, salt and sugar. Cook another minute, and serve.

Serving Suggestion: This vegetable dish would compliment a meat dish, such as **STEAMED PORK CAKE** or **BLACK BEAN SPARERIBS.**

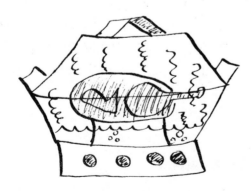

STIR-FRIED BOK CHOY
(Chow Bok Choy)

Serves 4

1	bunch bok choy (about ¾ lb.)	½ t.	thin soy sauce
1 T.	oil	1 T.	cornstarch
½ t.	salt	3 T.	cold water
½ t.	sugar		

1. Break branches off center stock of bok choy, removing and discarding any flowers.
2. Peel outer covering off center stock; then cut diagonally into 2" pieces.
3. Cut off and discard ¼" from the stem end of each leaf where it was attached to the center stock. Then, cut stems and leaves into 2" lengths.
4. Heat wok, add oil and stir-fry bok choy for 3 minutes; add salt, sugar and soy sauce.
5. Mix cornstarch with water, stir into vegetable, bring to a boil, and serve.

Serving Suggestion: Serve with SWEET AND SOUR PORK, HAM WITH BEAN THREADS, and STEAMED EGGS.

STUFFED BEAN CAKES
(Yeung Dow Foo)

Serves 4

¼ lb.   fresh prawns
8   Chinese mushrooms, small
¼ lb.   ground pork
1   green onion, chopped
1 pkg.   soy bean cake (Tofu)*
3 T.   oil

SEASONING

½ t. salt
½ t. sugar
1 t. thin soy sauce
¾ t. oyster sauce
     dash of pepper
¾ T. cornstarch

SAUCE

1 T. bean sauce (canned)
1 T. thin soy sauce
1 T. white wine
1 t. sugar
¾ C. chicken stock

1. Shell, devein, wash and mince prawns.

2. Boil mushrooms for 10 minutes, rinse, squeeze dry, cut off and discard stems; then, chop into very small pieces.

3. Place prawns, mushrooms, pork and green onion on the chopping board. Mix and chop for about 15 strokes.

4. Add "seasoning" and mix well.

5. Cut bean cake into two layers; cut each layer into 6 equal cubes (**approx. 1½"**).

6. Make a pocket by slitting and removing a small amount of bean cake so as to form a pocket in each cube.

7. Stuff the bean cakes with the mixture.

8. Rinse bean sauce once and crush with the handle of the cleaver. Add remaining sauce ingredients and mix thoroughly. Set aside.

9. Heat wok, add 1½ T. oil and pan-fry 6 stuffed bean cakes. Fry the meat side first for 3 minutes. Brown the remaining sides for two minutes each. Repeat this procedure using the remaining bean cakes and oil.

10. Place bean cakes in the wok, add bean sauce mixture and bring to a boil. Cover, cook for 5 minutes, and serve.

*Be sure to buy the porous type bean cake as the smooth type is too soft to stuff.

Continued

STUFFED BEAN CAKES, STEAMED
(Jing Yeung Dow Foo)

Variation I

12	stuffed bean cakes	½ t.	sugar
1 T.	bean sauce (canned)		dash of pepper
1	green onion, chopped	1½ T.	oil
2 t.	thin soy sauce		

1. Place the stuffed bean cakes in a shallow dish or pie pan.
2. Rinse bean sauce once and crush with the handle of the cleaver.
3. Add remaining ingredients, except oil and green onion, to the crushed bean sauce and mix well.
4. Cover the bean cakes with the bean sauce mixture.
5. Sprinkle chopped green onion on top.
6. Pour oil over the bean cakes.
7. Cover and steam for 15 minutes. **(See STEAMING HINTS)**

STUFFED BEAN CAKES IN BROTH
(Yeung Dow Foo Tong)

Variation II

12 stuffed bean cakes	¼ head lettuce	3 C. chicken stock

1. Cut lettuce into 1" wedges.
2. Bring chicken stock to a boil.
3. Add bean cakes and lettuce. Cover and cook for 5 minutes.

BEEF CHOW MEIN
(Ngow Yuk Chow Mein)

FOR PAN-FRYING NOODLES:

1 lb.	noodles*
6 T.	oil
1½ t.	dark soy sauce
	dash of salt

MARINADE

1 t.	salt	1 t.	thin soy sauce
¾ t.	sugar	1 t.	oyster sauce
	dash of pepper	1 T.	cornstarch
		1	green onion, chopped

BEEF MIXTURE

1·lb.	flank steak	½ t.	salt	2 t.	water
3	stalks celery	½ t.	sugar	1½ t.	oyster sauce
1 lb.	bean sprouts	¾ C.	chicken stock	½ t.	thin soy sauce
3 T.	oil	1 t.	cornstarch		

PROCEDURE FOR NOODLES

1. Bring 2 quarts of water to a boil, add 1/3 of the noodles and cook for 2 minutes. **(If you use dried noodles, cook them for 5 minutes.)** While noodles are boiling, heat the frying pan and add 2 T. oil. Remove noodles from water, drain well, and immediately put noodles in hot frying pan, adding ½ t. dark soy sauce and mixing thoroughly; then flatten them to form a large pancake. Pan-fry for 5 minutes over low to medium heat; turn noodles, sprinkle them with a little salt and pan-fry the other side for 5 minutes.

2. Repeat step 1 with each of the remaining portions of noodles.

3. Break each noodle pancake into about 10 parts and set aside.

*Either fresh or dried noodles may be used in preparing pan-fried noodles.

Continued

Beef Chow Mein (Continued)

PROCEDURE FOR BEEF MIXTURE

1. Cut flank steak into 3 long strips **(with the grain of the meat)**. Cut each strip into thin slices, cutting across the grain.
2. Sprinkle meat with each of the ingredients listed under "marinade", mix well and marinate for 1 hour.
3. Cut celery into 1½" pieces; then, cut each piece lengthwise into strips, julienne style.
4. Heat wok, add 1 T. oil and stir-fry the celery and bean sprouts for 3 minutes, adding ½ t. salt, and ½ t. sugar, and set aside.
5. Heat wok, add 2 T. oil and stir-fry marinated beef for 3 minutes.
6. Add the chicken stock and bring it to a boil.
7. Add thickening made from mixing 1 t. cornstarch with 2 t. cold water. Cook for 1 minute.
8. Add celery mixture.
9. Remove half of the mixture from the wok and set aside, adding to the wok ½ of the pan-fried noodles, ¾ t. oyster sauce, and ¼ t. thin soy sauce. Mix well **(approximately 3 min.)** and set aside.
10. Place the remaining noodles, meat mixture, oyster sauce and thin soy sauce in the wok, mixing for approximately 3 minutes. Then add it to the mixture which was previously set aside, and serve.

Note: Left over **BEEF CHOW MEIN** can be kept in the refrigerator for several days. Wrap in foil and heat in a 325 degree oven for about 15 minutes.

CHICKEN CHOW MEIN
(Gai Chow Mein)

Serves 6

FOR PAN-FRIED NOODLES:

1 lb.	fresh noodles
6 T.	oil
1½ t.	dark soy sauce
	dash of salt

- -

1	whole chicken breast (approx. 12 ozs.)
¾ lb.	cabbage, shredded
1	small can sliced mushrooms
2 T.	oil
½ C.	water

SEASONING

½ t.	salt
½ t.	sugar
½ t.	thin soy sauce
1 t.	oyster sauce
1 t.	cornstarch
	dash of pepper

THICKENING

2 t.	cornstarch
1½ T.	water
1 t.	thin soy sauce
1 t.	oyster sauce

1. For pan-frying noodles, see **BEEF CHOW MEIN** (page 128).

2. Skin and bone chicken; cut into 1½" x ½" pieces.

3. Add "seasoning" and mix well.

4. Heat wok, add 1 T. oil, and stir-fry cabbage and mushrooms for 3 minutes. Remove and set aside.

5. Heat wok, add 1 T. oil, and stir-fry chicken for 3 minutes; add water, cover, and cook for 3 minutes more.

6. Add cabbage mixture and thickening, made from ingredients listed under "thickening". Cook for 1 minute.

7. Remove one-half of the mixture and add one-half of the noodles. Mix thoroughly **(approximately 3 min.)** and set aside.

8. Place the remaining noodles and chicken mixture in the wok, mixing for approximately 3 minutes. Then add to the mixture which was previously set aside, and serve.

CHICKEN TOPPING ON NOODLES
(Gai Kow Mein)

2	whole chicken breasts
25	snow peas
1	small can sliced mushrooms
1 lb.	fresh egg noodles
1¼ T.	oil (approx.)
1 C.	water
1 T.	dark soy sauce
1½ T.	cornstarch
3 T.	cold water

SEASONING

1 t.	salt
1 t.	sugar
1 t.	thin soy sauce
1 t.	white wine
1 T.	oyster sauce
	dash of pepper
1 T.	cornstarch
2	green onions, slivered

BROTH

8 C.	water
	chicken bones from breasts
2	chicken bouillon cubes
¼ t.	dark soy sauce
½ t.	salt

1. Bone chicken breasts and cut into strips 1½" x ½" x ¼".

2. Add "seasoning" to chicken and mix well.

3. Snap off the stem end of the snow peas; then cut diagonally into two pieces.

4. Prepare chicken broth by cooking ingredients listed under "broth" for 15 minutes. Keep hot over low heat until ready to use.

5. Bring 3 quarts of water to a boil in a large saucepan; then add noodles, stirring to prevent them from sticking. Cook for 5 minutes. Run under cold water and drain. Set noodles aside.

6. Heat wok and add 1 t. oil. Stir-fry snow peas for 3 minutes over medium heat. Stir often, as they burn very easily. Sprinkle with a little salt and sugar and set aside.

Continued

Chicken Topping On Noodles (Continued)

7.   Heat wok, add 1 T. oil, and stir-fry the chicken for 5 minutes.

8.   Add 1 C. water, 1 T. dark soy sauce and sliced mushrooms. Bring to a boil.

9.   Add thickening made with 1½ T. cornstarch and 3 T. cold water.

10. Add the stir-fried snow peas.

11. Add noodles to the chicken stock and bring to a fast boil. Put in a large serving bowl, place chicken and snow peas on top and serve.

Note: Noodles can be cooked a few hours earlier.

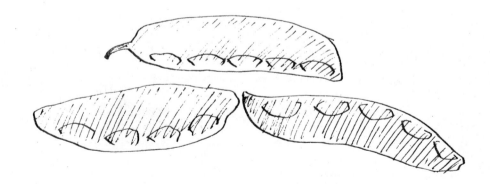

NOODLES IN GRAVY
(Yee Mein)

Serves 6

20	small Chinese mushrooms (or 1 can sliced mushrooms)	½ lb.	bean sprouts
¼ lb.	Chinese barbecued pork	2	green onions, slivered
½ lb.	bok choy	½ t.	salt
1 pkg.	pre-fried noodles (½ lb.)	½ t.	sugar
1 qt.	chicken stock	2 T.	oyster sauce
3 T.	oil	1 t.	cornstarch
		2 t.	water

1. Cook Chinese mushrooms by boiling in water for 10 minutes. Rinse, squeeze dry, remove and discard stems; cut mushrooms into strips, julienne style.
2. Cut barbecued pork into very thin slices.
3. Break branches off center stock of bok choy. Remove and discard any flowers. Peel outer covering off center stock. Cut bok choy diagonally into 2" lengths.
4. Bring chicken stock to a boil, add noodles, and cook for 5 min. Drain and set aside. Discard the stock, as it will be quite oily!
5. Heat wok, add 1 T. oil and stir-fry bok choy, bean sprouts, green onions, barbecued pork, and mushrooms for 3 minutes, adding ½ t. salt and ½ t. sugar. Remove and set aside.
6. Heat wok, add 2 T. oil and noodles. Stir-fry for 2 minutes; then, add the oyster sauce. Mix well.
7. Add all other ingredients, **except** cornstarch and 2 t. water, and toss together until well mixed.
8. Add thickening made by mixing the cornstarch with the cold water. Cook for 1 minute, and serve.

Serving Suggestion: Serve as a plate luncheon or with other dishes for dinner.

NOODLES IN OYSTER SAUCE
(Gon Lo Mein)

Serves 5

1 qt.	water	2 T.	oyster sauce
1 lb.	fresh noodles (or dried noodles)	1	green onion, chopped
1 T.	oil (for stir-fry)	½ t.	salt
1 T.	sesame oil (for flavor)	2 t.	thin soy sauce

1. In a large saucepan bring 1 quart of water to a boil. Add noodles and stir a little to prevent the noodles from sticking. Cook for 5 minutes. **If dried noodles are used,** cook for 10 minutes. Remove from heat, run under cold water **(as you do with spaghetti)** and drain well.

2. Heat wok and add 1 T. oil; then add noodles and stir-fry for 3 minutes. Add remaining ingredients to noodles, mixing well, and serve.

Serving Suggestion: Serve for lunch with a garnish of chopped ham or Chinese barbecued pork.

SPICED NOODLES
(Ja Jeung Mein)

1	Chinese mustard pickle (¾ C.)*	2 T.	oil
1/8 lb.	Chinese barbecued pork	¼ lb.	lean ground pork
1 T.	bean sauce (canned)	2/3 C.	chicken stock
3 qts.	water	1 T.	Tabasco pepper sauce OR
1 lb.	fresh egg noodles		chili paste with garlic
½ lb.	bean sprouts	1 t.	cornstarch
1	green onion, chopped	2 t.	cold water

1. Cut pickle into pea-size bits and soak for 10 minutes in warm water. Rinse and drain.
2. Cut barbecued pork into thin strips, julienne style.
3. Rinse bean sauce once and mash with the handle of the cleaver.
4. Bring 3 quarts of water to a boil, add noodles and cook for 5 minutes. Rinse noodles under cold water, drain, and set aside.
5. Heat wok, add 1 T. oil and stir-fry bean sprouts, mustard pickles, chopped green onion, and barbecued pork for 2 minutes. Sprinkle·lightly with salt and sugar. Remove and set aside.
6. Reheat wok, add 1 T. oil, bean sauce, and ground pork. Stir-fry for 2 minutes.
7. Add chicken stock and pepper sauce. Cover and cook for 8 minutes.
8. Add bean sprout mixture and bring to a fast boil.
9. Prepare thickening made with the cornstarch and cold water. Add thickening to the meat mixture, and cook for 1 minute.
10. Add noodles to the meat mixture, mix thoroughly, and serve.

Variations: You can substitute baked ham for the barbecued pork, and cabbage for bean sprouts.

*Chinese mustard pickles come in a can. They are spicy. Remaining pickles will keep in the refrigerator for several months.

TOMATO BEEF CHOW MEIN
(Fon Kerr Ngow Yuk Chow Mein)

Serves 8

FOR PAN-FRYING NOODLES:

1 lb.	fresh noodles
6 T.	oil
1½ t.	dark soy sauce
	dash of salt

SEASONING

1 t.	salt
½ t.	sugar
1 t.	thin soy sauce
1 t.	oyster sauce
1 T.	cornstarch
	dash of pepper

BEEF MIXTURE:

1 lb.	flank steak	2 T.	oil	
2	stalks celery	¾ T.	cornstarch	
½	yellow onion	1½ T.	cold water	
1	bell pepper			
2	tomatoes			

SAUCE

½ C.	water
1 T.	apple cider vinegar
2 t.	catsup
¼ t.	salt
¼ t.	thin soy sauce
2 T.	sugar

PROCEDURE FOR NOODLES

1. Bring 2 quarts of water to a boil, add 1/3 of the noodles and cook for 2 minutes. **(If you use dried noodles, cook them for 5 minutes.)** While noodles are boiling, heat the frying pan and add 2 T. oil. Remove noodles from water, drain well, and immediately put noodles in hot frying pan, adding ½ t. dark soy sauce and mixing thoroughly; then flatten them to form a large pancake. Pan-fry for 5 minutes over low-medium heat; turn noodles, sprinkle them with a little salt and pan-fry the other side for 5 minutes.

2. Repeat step 1. with each of the remaining portions of noodles.

3. Break each noodle pancake into about 10 parts and set aside.

Continued

Tomato Beef Chow Mein (Continued)

PROCEDURE FOR BEEF MIXTURE

1. Cut flank steak into 3 long strips **(with the grain of the meat)**. Cut each strip into thin slices, cutting across the grain. Add "seasoning" and mix well.

2. Cut celery into 1½" pieces; then cut each piece lengthwise into strips, julienne style.

3. Cut yellow onion into 5 wedges.

4. Remove seeds from bell pepper and then cut into 1" pieces.

5. Cut tomatoes into 8 equal parts.

6. Heat wok, add 1 T. oil and stir-fry celery, onion and bell pepper for 2 minutes, sprinkling lightly with salt and sugar. Remove and set aside.

7. Heat wok, add 1 T. oil and stir-fry beef for 3 minutes. Remove and set aside.

8. Put the ingredients listed under "sauce" into the wok and bring it to a boil over high heat. When boiling, add tomato, beef and vegetables. Mix thoroughly, and bring to a fast boil again.

9. Thicken slightly with a mixture made from ¾ T. cornstarch and 1½ T. cold water. Cook for 1 minute.

10. Remove half of the mixture from wok and set it aside. Add ½ the pan-fried noodles and mix thoroughly **(approx. 3 min.)**, and set aside.

11. Place the remaining noodles and meat mixture in the wok, mixing for approx. 3 minutes. Then add it to the mixture which was previously set aside, and serve.

FRIED RICE
(Chow Fon)

Serves 6

4	eggs, beaten	4 T.	oil
1½ C.	shredded lettuce (Iceberg)	4 C.	cooked rice
¾ C.	frozen peas, defrosted	1 t.	salt
¼ lb.	Chinese barbecued pork, diced	1 T.	oyster sauce
1	green onion, chopped	1 t.	dark soy sauce

1. Heat wok, add 1 T. oil, and scramble the eggs. Remove and set aside.

2. Heat wok, add ½ T. oil and stir-fry peas, barbecued pork and green onion for 2 minutes. Set aside.

3. Heat wok, add 2½ T. oil and the rice. Stir-fry for 10 minutes. **(If you are using leftover rice and the rice is hard, add 2 t. water to soften it.) Use medium-low heat** and be sure to stir constantly as the rice burns easily.

4. Add salt, oyster sauce and dark soy sauce, mixing thoroughly.

5. Add all other ingredients and mix thoroughly again.

Note: Fried rice is the Chinese equivalent of "Mulligan Stew". Into it can go almost anything that may be left over.

Serving Suggestion: Serve fried rice with any Chinese dish for dinner or as a one dish plate lunch or dinner.

STEAMED RICE
(Bok Fon)

Serves 3

3 C. raw rice* (long grain)
3 C. cold water

1. Put rice in the pot and wash it thoroughly 3 to 4 times in cold water. Drain off excess water.
2. Add the cold water to the rice, cover and bring it to a boil. Cook about 7 - 8 minutes at high heat.
3. Remove cover and continue cooking for about 5 minutes more (**until water is absorbed**).
4. Cover and simmer for 10 minutes more over low flame. Be very careful at this point as the rice burns very easily. If the rice is accidentally scorched, it may be salvaged by placing a piece of bread in the pot to absorb the burnt flavor. (**Throw away the bread!**)

Note: Chinese people have a different way of measuring the amount of water they use when preparing rice. They usually use enough water to cover the first joint of the middle finger when it is just touching the rice. The water will be about 1 inch above the rice. No matter how much rice you use, the water should be about 1 inch above the rice. (**When using an electric rice cooker, only use ¾" of water above the rice OR follow directions given with the cooker.**)

Incidentally . . . . . .
1. Salt is never used when preparing "steamed rice".
2. Chinese people usually wash their rice before using it.
3. If you use "pre-cooked" packaged rice, follow the directions on the package.

*1 cup of raw rice equals 2 cups of cooked rice.

SWEET RICE
(Gnaw Mai Fon)

Serves 6

3 C.	sweet rice*	1 T.	oil
2	Chinese sausages	3 T.	water
10	Chinese mushrooms, small	1 T.	thin soy sauce
1/3 C.	dried shrimp	1 T.	oyster sauce
1	green onion, chopped		

1. Prepare rice according to **STEAMED RICE** recipe (See page 139).

2. Steam Chinese sausage for 20 minutes; then dice into small pieces.

3. Boil Chinese mushrooms for 10 minutes, rinse, squeeze dry, cut off and discard stems; then dice into small pieces.

4. Soak dried shrimp in warm water for 5 minutes. Rinse and drain.

5. Heat wok, add oil and stir-fry dried shrimp for 1 minute. Add the 3 T. water and simmer for about 2 minutes **(until the liquid has been absorbed)**.

6. Add mushrooms, Chinese sausage and green onion. Stir-fry for 1 minute and remove from the wok.

7. Put cooked rice in a deep pan. Add soy sauce and oyster sauce and mix thoroughly.

8. Add sausage mixture, mix thoroughly, and serve.

Serving Suggestions: Serve as a one-dish dinner or as a turkey dressing in place of a regular bread dressing.

Variations: Chinese barbecued pork or cooked ham may be substituted for the Chinese sausages and ½ C. sliced mushrooms may be substituted for the Chinese mushrooms.

*Buy sweet rice at an Oriental grocery store or in the gourmet section of your favorite super-market.

BASIC WON TON
(Won Ton Haum)

10	Chinese mushrooms, small	1 t.	salt
¼ lb.	raw prawns	½ t.	sugar
5	fresh water chestnuts (or 7 canned ones)*	1 t.	thin soy sauce
½ lb.	ground pork	1 t.	oyster sauce
1	green onion, finely chopped		dash of pepper
1 pkg.	won ton skins (contains 80)**	1¼ T.	cornstarch
		1	egg, small

1. Boil Chinese mushrooms for 10 minutes, rinse, squeeze dry, cut off and discard stems; then, chop into very small pieces.

2. Shell, devein and wash prawns. Chop into very small pieces.

3. Peel and crush water chestnuts with the flat side of the cleaver. If you don't have a cleaver, chop the water chestnuts into very fine pieces.

4. Combine mushrooms, prawns, water chestnuts, pork and green onion.

5. Add all other ingredients and mix well. 1 teaspoon of filling is used for each won ton.

See next page for directions for wrapping won ton.

Note: Won Ton may be wrapped a few hours in advance or they will keep in a covered container in the freezer for 3 - 4 weeks.

*If you use canned water chestnuts, stir-fry them with 1 t. oil for 1 - 2 minutes, adding 1 t. sugar. Let cool before using.

**Won ton skins can be frozen for 2 months if put in a plastic bag or they will keep in the refrigerator for one week.

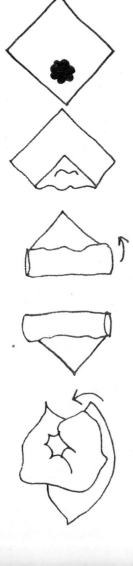

HOW TO WRAP WON TON
(Bau Won Ton)

1. With one corner of the skin toward you, place 1 t. of filling about an inch from the corner.

2. Fold one corner to cover the filling.

3. Fold once more . . . about ¾".

4. Turn the won ton so that the triangle is toward you. Dampen the left corner with a little water.

5. Swing the right corner away from you and place it on top of the dampened left corner. As you make this fold, simultaneously pull the filling toward you with your middle finger. You should finish with a "hat-like" effect.

DEEP FRIED WON TON
(Jow Won Ton)

Makes 40

40   won ton (See Page 141)
1 qt. oil for deep-frying

1.   Heat oil to 325 degrees, and deep-fry won ton for 10 minutes. Remove and drain off excess oil. They can be fried a few hours ahead of serving time and kept at room temperature until just before serving. Reheat in oven at 275 degrees for 8 minutes.

Serving Suggestions: Fried won ton are delicious served as appetizers or they may be served with a sweet and sour sauce as one course in a Chinese dinner.

SWEET AND SOUR SAUCE DIP

1 C. water	¼ t. thin soy sauce
1/3 C. cider vinegar	1 T. catsup
½ C. sugar	2 T. cornstarch
1/8 t. salt	2 T. water

1.   Bring all ingredients, **except** cornstarch and 2 T. water, to a fast boil.

2.   Make thickening using the cornstarch and water. Add this to the mixture and cook for 1 minute, stirring continually.

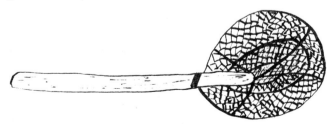

CHINESE STRAINER

WON TON IN GRAVY
(Mun Yee Won Ton)

Serves 4

40	won ton (See Page 141)
5 C.	chicken stock
½ C.	Chinese barbecued pork or ham, diced
1	green onion, chopped
1	can sliced mushrooms (optional)
1 C.	frozen peas, defrosted
2	egg whites, beaten

THICKENING MIXTURE

2½ T.	cornstarch
5 T.	cold water
1½ t.	dark soy sauce
1 t.	sesame oil

- -

1 qt.	oil for deep-frying

1. Heat oil to 325 degrees and deep-fry won ton for 10 minutes. Remove and drain off excess oil. Won ton can be fried a few hours ahead of serving time and kept at room temperature until just before using.

2. Bring chicken stock to a fast boil; add all of the remaining ingredients in the left hand column **excepting the egg whites** and including the won ton. Boil for 3 minutes.

3. Add the egg whites and stir well.

4. Mix ingredients listed under "Thickening Mixture," add to the broth, cook for 1 minute, and serve.

Serving Suggestions: Serve as a one dish lunch or serve with **CHINESE STRING BEANS WITH PRAWNS** and **STEAMED RICE** for a satisfying dinner.

WON TON IN OYSTER SAUCE
(Ho Yau Gon Lo Won Ton)

Serves 4

40 **won ton (See Page 141)**	**1 T. thin soy sauce**
2 qts. **water**	**2 T. oyster sauce**
1½ T. **sesame oil**	**1** **green onion, chopped**

1. In a large saucepan bring 2 qts. water to a boil.

2. Add won ton and boil for 5 minutes; then, remove with a Chinese strainer or colander.

3. Put the cooked won ton in a deep serving bowl, add all other ingredients except the green onion, and mix carefully.

4. Garnish with the chopped green onion.

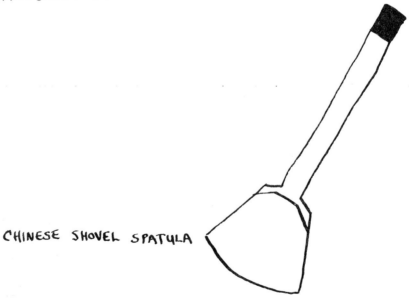

CHINESE SHOVEL SPATULA

WON TON SOUP
(Tong Won Ton)

Serves 4

40 won ton (See page 141)
 2 qts. water

BROTH INGREDIENTS

5 C. chicken stock
2 C. shredded lettuce

Optional - thin slices of any leftover meats may be added (barbecued pork, chicken, ham, etc.)

1. Prepare the soup by adding broth ingredients. Bring to a boil, and keep warm.

2. In a large separate container, bring the water to a boil. Add the won ton and cook for 8 - 10 minutes. **(Be sure to use a sufficiently large container so that the won ton will not stick together.)** Stir occasionally while cooking.

3. Using strainer or colander, remove the won ton from the water.

4. Divide the won ton equally into 4 individual serving bowls. Ladle the hot soup over the won ton.

Condiments: Use small individual condiment dishes containing a mixture of 1 t. soy sauce and 1 t. oyster sauce. Chinese hot mustard or hot sauce may be used for a spicier taste!

Note: With a little imagination, you will find that almost any green leafy vegetable may be used to add color and taste to the soup.

ALMOND MILK CURD
(Hung Yun Dow Foo)

Serves 4

1 C.	cold water
1	envelope Knox gelatin
½ C.	sugar

1 T.	almond extract
1 C.	milk
1	small can Mandarin oranges, chilled

1. Put the cold water in a saucepan and slowly add the gelatin.
2. Stir constantly, over medium heat, for 3 minutes.
3. Add sugar, almond extract, and milk. Mix thoroughly, and cook for 1 minute.
4. Pour mixture in a pyrex dish. Refrigerate until firm (**approx. 6 hrs.**).
5. After the milk curd is firm, cut it into inch cubes and put in individual serving dishes.
6. Garnish each serving with slices of mandarin oranges. Use 1 t. of the fruit syrup also.

Variations: Any kind of canned fruit may be substituted. **However,** if you would like a real taste treat, try substituting canned loquats, longans (**dragon's eyes**), or Li-chees in place of the mandarin oranges. These are available in any Oriental grocery store or in the foreign foods section of your favorite supermarket.

Another delicious variation is achieved by sprinkling sweetened grated coconut over the top of the milk curd.

BARBECUED PORK BUN
(Cha Siu Bow)

Makes 16 buns

DOUGH

1/3 C.	warm water
½ t.	sugar
1 pkg.	dry yeast
2½ C.	flour
2½ C.	cake flour
4 T.	sugar
½ t.	salt
2 T.	shortening
1¼ C.	milk
16	pieces white paper 2" sq.*

FILLING

6 ozs.	Chinese barbecued pork, diced
1 T.	oil
2 T.	water
½ t.	salt
½ t.	sugar
½ t.	thin soy sauce
1 t.	oyster sauce
1 t.	hoisin sauce
2 t.	cornstarch
4 t.	cold water (for thickening)

1. Mix together the warm water, ½ t. sugar and yeast in an 8 oz. measuring cup. Let stand until it rises to the 8 oz. level **(about 20 minutes)**.

2. Sift flour, cake flour, sugar and salt into a large mixing bowl.

3. Add shortening, yeast mixture and milk.

4. Knead mixture 5 minutes to form a dough. Cover with a damp cloth and set dough in a warm place. Allow the dough to rise for 3 hours.

5. Heat wok, add oil and stir-fry pork for 2 minutes.

6. Add 2 T. water, salt, sugar, soy sauce, oyster sauce and hoisin sauce. Bring it to a boil.

7. Prepare thickening by mixing the cornstarch and 4 t. cold water. Stir into the mixture and cook for 1 minute. Let cool before using.

8. After 3 hours, when the dough has risen, shape into rolls about 2" in diameter. Cut each roll into 1½" pieces.

*Use any white paper that is not waxed.

Continued

Barbecued Pork Bun (Continued)

9. Shape each piece into a shallow bowl shape.
10. Put 1 T. filling in the center, close and twist dough to form a bun. Put the bun on a 2" square of white paper. **(This prevents the bun from becoming soggy while steaming.)** Place 8 buns in a pie pan and allow them to set and rise for 15 minutes in a warm place.
11. Steam for 25 minutes. See "Steaming Hints".

Note: Steamed **CHA SIU BOWS** may be kept in the refrigerator for 1 week. If frozen, they will keep for months. To serve just reheat by steaming for 10 minutes.

See diagram on following page.

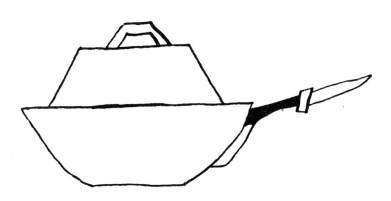

SHAPING A PORK BUN

1.   SPOON FILLING ONTO DOUGH.

2.   GATHER EDGES OF DOUGH
AROUND FILLING.

3.   TWIST FOLDS OF DOUGH
TOGETHER AT TOP.

FRESH COCONUT AND PRESERVED SWEET AND SOUR GINGER
(Yeh Gee Tim-Sheun Gerng)

1   fresh coconut
    preserved sweet and sour ginger (in jar)*

1. Husk and crack coconut shell. This may be done by piercing the "eyes" of the coconut, removing the milk by shaking the coconut, and either breaking the shell with a hammer, sawing the shell in half, or by heating the coconut in the oven **(temperature 325 degrees)** for 30 minutes. **(The heat will crack the shell.)**

2. Remove the brown covering on the coconut meat.

3. Cut the coconut meat into strips for easy eating.

Note: A bite of coconut first and a **small** bite of ginger combine to give a very delicious taste treat. It is not only delicious but good for the digestion!

*"Sweet and Sour Ginger" comes already prepared and can be bought in a Chinese grocery store or in the "Foreign Foods" section of many stores. The unused ginger will keep several months if kept in the refrigerator.

HOT SPICED OIL
(Laht Yau)

4 dried chili peppers	½ C. oil
OR	
2 t. crushed dried chili peppers	

1. Rinse whole chili peppers, dry thoroughly, and crush.

2. Put in a glass container, add oil, cover and let stand 1 to 2 weeks during which time the crushed chili pepper will settle to the bottom of the jar.

Note: This oil will keep at room temperature for several months. If whole dried chili peppers are used, the oil will have a more colorful appearance.

Serving Suggestions: Use as a condiment **(using equal parts of spiced oil and soy sauce)** as well as in seasoning meat, if you enjoy "spicy" dishes.

Variation: Substitute soy sauce for the oil and use in the same manner.

MANDARIN GLAZED APPLE AND BANANA
(But See Ping Gwo Herng Jiu)

Serves 4

2 T.	sesame seeds
1	banana (med. size)
1	apple (med. size)
3 C.	ice cold water

- -

1½ C. oil (for deep-frying)

BATTER

1	egg (large)
3 T.	cornstarch
3 T.	flour
2 T.	cold water

GLAZE

9 T.	sugar
2 T.	Karo corn syrup*
2 T.	cold water

1. Toast the sesame seeds in a saucepan for 2 minutes. **DON'T USE OIL!**
2. Peel banana and cut into five pieces.
3. Peel and core apple. Cut into 8 pieces.
4. Prepare the batter by beating the egg, adding the cornstarch, flour and water. Mix well.
5. While the oil is heating to 325 degrees, prepare the glaze by mixing the sugar, corn syrup and water and cooking it over medium flame for about 4 min. Be sure to stir the syrup occasionally to prevent burning. Keep warm over low heat.
6. Dip several pieces of fruit into the batter and then deep-fry them for approx. 2 minutes. Remove and drain off excess oil.
7. Immediately dip the deep-fried fruit into the glaze and put on a plate.
8. Sprinkle with toasted sesame seeds and immediately dip the fruit in ice cold water. Remove and put on a serving dish.

Variation: Pears may be substituted for apples or bananas.

*Be sure to buy **light** corn syrup.

153

MONGOLIAN FIRE POT
(Dah Bien Loo)

Serves 4

1.	whole chicken breast (approx. 12 ozs.)
½ lb.	prawns
¼ lb.	ground pork
2	green onions
2	stalks celery
1 pkg.	bean cake
1	bunch spinach
¼	head lettuce
11 C.	chicken stock

SEASONING FOR CHICKEN

½ t. salt   ½ t. sugar

SEASONING FOR GROUND PORK:

½ t. salt
½ t. sugar
¾ t. thin soy sauce
   dash of pepper
1 t. cornstarch

DIPPING MIXTURE: (Prepare individual dishes, one for each guest.)

1 T. thin soy sauce   ½ t. sesame oil   dash of pepper

1. Skin and bone chicken. Cut into 1" by ½" pieces and put in a serving dish.
2. Add "seasoning" to chicken and mix well.
3. Shell, devein, wash and drain prawns. Put in a shallow serving dish.
4. Add "seasoning" to ground pork and mix well. Shape into meat balls (about 1" in diameter), and put in a serving dish.
5. Cut green onions into 1" pieces. Put in a shallow serving dish.
6. Cut celery into 2" pieces; then, cut each piece lengthwise into strips, julienne style. Put in a shallow serving dish.
7. Drain bean cake and cut into 1" cubes. Put in a serving dish.
8. Clean spinach, cut off and discard ½" from stem end and break into 2" pieces. Put in a deep serving bowl.
9. Rinse lettuce and break into 2" pieces, and put in a deep serving bowl.

Continued

10. Arrange the dishes of food on the table so that they surround the "fire pot". Each guest will have his own bowl, a small individual dish of the "dipping mixture", 2 pairs of chopsticks **(one pair for removing food from the fire pot and the other pair for eating purposes)** as well as an individual Chinese strainer.

11. In a deep-fryer, Japanese rice cooker, or electric skillet, put 11 cups of chicken stock and bring it to a boil.

12. The food of your choice will be put in your strainer and carefully held in the broth for the approximate amount of time listed below.

     Celery, spinach, lettuce, green onions & bean cake require about 2 minutes.

     Chicken and prawns require 3 minutes.

     Meatballs require about 4 minutes.

Note: Thinly sliced flank steak, fish cakes, squid, napa cabbage, watercress, or bok choy may be substituted for any ingredients listed above. Cook for 3 minutes.

This is a fun "party" recipe, which invites each guest to do his own thing, whatever suits his fancy or taste. He may choose fowl, meat, or vegetable, cook each to his own degree of taste, and eat as much as he chooses. The fun may even begin in the kitchen, where each is invited to prepare one or more of the items to be set on the table. And, this dish challenges the imagination; what else might be added to the firepot?

Historically, this recipe is a favored one for the cold of Winter. The original firepots burned briquets, or charcoal. Thus, the heat from the brazier warmed one externally, while the hot food warmed one internally.

Incidentally, after the "goodies" are cooked in the chicken broth, do not hesitate to drink the soup.

NEW YEAR'S CAKE
(Nien Goh)

Serves 8

1 lb.   brown sugar bars, Chinese
1½ C.   cold water

1 lb.   glutinous rice powder
2 T.   vegetable oil

1. Dissolve sugar bars in the cold water, by letting it stand overnight, or by stirring continuously over low heat.

2. Put rice flour into a large mixing bowl. Add the sugar syrup. Using a spoon, mix thoroughly for 5 minutes.

3. Now add the oil; mix well.

4. Oil a 9" cake pan. Pour in the flour mixture.

5. Steam for 3 hours. **BE SURE TO CHECK WATER LEVEL EVERY HALF HOUR!**

Note: **NEW YEAR'S CAKE** is not served immediately. It must 'set' for 15 to 24 hours. The Chinese cook this prior to New Year's Day. The New Year's Cake, decorated with a couple of oranges or tangerines and red envelopes containing offerings of money, is generally placed in the kitchen. It is food for the kitchen god.

Serving Suggestions: Cut into 2 inch wedges and serve it cold, hot, or fried. When served hot, steam for 10 minutes. If fried, use a teflon frying pan, without oil. Fry 2 minutes on each side over low heat. The inside of the cake will become soft and hot, while the outside has a nice brown crust. Hot tea is usually served with New Year's Cake.

Variation: After the cake has steamed for 2¾ hours, sprinkle 3 tablespoons of shredded coconut over the top; then, continue steaming for 15 more minutes.

PICKLED CARROTS AND DAIKON RADISH
(Sheun Law Bok)

1½ lbs. daikon radish (12" - 14" long)
2   carrots
1½ C.   cold water

¾ C.   apple cider vinegar
1 C.   sugar
1¼ t.   salt

1. Prepare pickling brine by combining water, cider vinegar, sugar and ½ t. salt in an enamel pot, bring to a boil and set aside to cool.

2. Peel radish and carrots; cut diagonally into thin slices and put in separate containers.

3. Put radish slices in a colander, sprinkle with ¾ t. salt, mix, and let stand for a couple of hours.

4. Squeeze moisture out of radish slices as this removes any bitterness they might have. Run cold water over the radish slices while you shake them several times; then squeeze out as much water as possible.

5. Put radish and carrots in a quart jar and pour in enough brine to fill the jar. Let stand at room temperature for 2 days before serving, but keep in the refrigerator after 2 days...just as you do regular pickles.

Note: You can prepare cucumbers the same way! Peel lengthwise to form stripes; next cut cucumbers in half, lengthwise, remove seeds and cut into thin slices. Then follow the regular procedure for the **PICKLED CARROTS AND DAIKON RADISH.**

PICKLED MUSTARD GREENS
(Sheum Guy Choy)

Serves 6

1½ lbs.	Chinese mustard greens		1¼ C.	sugar
1 C.	apple cider vinegar		½ t.	salt
1½ C.	cold water		1 t.	thin soy sauce

1. Prepare pickling brine by combining vinegar, water, sugar, salt and thin soy sauce in an enamel pot, bring to a boil and set aside to cool.
2. Break branches off center stock of Chinese mustard greens. Cut into 1" pieces.
3. Peel outer covering off center stock; then cut into pieces 1½" x ¾".
4. Rinse mustard greens thoroughly, drain and then put in a glass or enamel container.
5. Pour brine over mustard greens, cover and let stand for 3 days before eating.

Note: Pickled mustard greens will keep in the refrigerator for about 2 months.

Variation: If you would prefer a more spicy and hot pickled mustard greens, add 4 chopped dried chili peppers to the pickling mixture.

POT STICKERS
(Huo Tip)

Makes 15

2½ C. flour
1 C. water
2 ozs. cabbage (approx. ½ C., cooked
     and chopped)
½ lb. lean ground pork
1 green onion, chopped
1 t. chopped ginger
3 T. oil
1 C. chicken stock

SEASONING

¼ t. salt
¼ t. sugar
1 t. thin soy sauce
1 t. oyster sauce
1 t. white wine
     dash of pepper
1 t. cornstarch

DIP

2 t. thin soy sauce
1 t. hot spiced oil (See page 152)
1 t. white vinegar

1. Combine flour and cold water in large mixing bowl. Mix thoroughly to form dough. Cover with damp cloth; let stand for 20 minutes.

2. Cook cabbage 2 minutes in boiling water. Rinse in cold water, and drain. Squeeze dry of all excess moisture. Chop fine; set aside.

3. Place the ground pork, chopped green onion, and chopped ginger together on chopping board. Mix and chop with the cleaver for approximately 12 strokes.

4. Add "seasoning" and the cabbage to the pork mixture and mix thoroughly.

5. After dough has set for 20 minutes, knead it for 1 minute and then form into 2 or 3 rolls, approximately 1½" in diameter. Cut each roll of dough into slices 1½" thick.

6. With a small rolling pin, or heel of hand, flatten each piece of dough into a thin patty, 3" in diameter. Place ¾ T. of the pork mixture in the center of each patty. Fold in half, and seal the edges by pressing firmly together with your fingers.

Continued

7. Set each pot sticker with the straight edge on a platter, pressing firmly so as to form a flat base. Each pot sticker should be made to stand upright, rather than allowed to rest flat on its side.

8. Heat wok, and add 1½ T. oil. Over medium heat, pan-fry 7 or 8 pot stickers. Cook on the base surface only. Pan-fry 2 to 3 minutes, until the base side is nicely browned.

9. Add ½ C. chicken stock to the pot stickers. Cover and cook over medium heat for approximately 7 minutes, until most of the chicken stock is absorbed. Remove to platter.

10. Repeat steps 8 and 9 with remaining pot stickers and chicken stock.

11. Mix thin soy sauce, hot spiced oil, and white vinegar to use as condiment for Pot Stickers..

Note: **POT STICKERS** are also called Kuo Teh. They will keep 3 to 4 days under refrigeration. Cooked pot stickers may be reheated by steaming for 7 minutes. Steam just prior to serving.

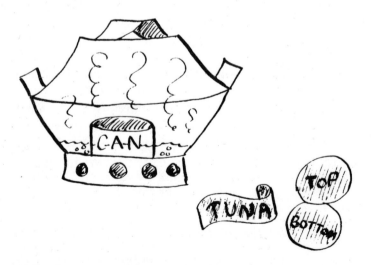

STEAMED PORK DUMPLINGS
(Shiu Mai)

Makes approx. 80

1 pkg.	round dumpling skins*	
½ lb.	prawns	
12	Chinese mushrooms, small	
½ lb.	ground pork	
1	green onion, finely chopped	
1	egg, small	

SEASONING

½ t. salt
1 t. sugar
½ t. sesame oil
2 t. thin soy sauce
1 T. cornstarch

1. Shell, devein, wash, and drain prawns. Dice into bits.

2. Boil mushrooms in water for 10 minutes, rinse, squeeze dry, cut off and discard stems; then, chop into very small pieces.

3. Combine the pork, mushrooms, prawns, and onion. Put mixture on chopping board and chop 10 to 15 strokes with the cleaver. **(Use a sharp knife if you don't have a cleaver.)** Texture, when you're finished, should be slightly finer than hamburger.

4. Add "seasoning" and the egg to the pork mixture. Mix well.

5. To make dumpling, place 1 T. filling in the center of a dumpling skin. Then bring all sides of the skin up to cover the meat as much as possible, without closing. The top of the dumpling is left open.

6. Cook dumplings by steaming for 30 minutes.

Note: After cooking, dumplings may be kept in the refrigerator for one week, in the freezer for 2 to 3 months. To serve just reheat by steaming for 10 minutes.

Serving Suggestion: Dumplings may be eaten hot or cold. Serve with soy sauce, hot sauce, or mustard.

*Dumpling skins are similar to **WON TON** skins...except that they are round and slightly thinner. You may substitute **WON TON** skins by merely cutting off the corners to round off the skin.

See diagram on following page.

SHAPING A PORK DUMPLING
(Ju Shiu Mai Fong Fat)

1. SPOON FILLING ONTO SKIN.

2. GATHER SKIN AROUND FILLING.

3. SQUEEZE CENTER TO PACK FILLING TIGHTLY.
    FLATTEN BOTTOM OF DUMPLING.

WHY NOT TRY A "YUM CHA" AT A CHINESE TEA LUNCH RESTAURANT?

YUM CHA, or "tea lunch", is always an expected pleasure for a Chinese family, particularly when the father is off from work, and the entire family can participate. It is exciting for many reasons: the family has an outing, the variety of dishes is very large **(and delicious),** and afterwards all may enjoy a leisurely stroll around Chinatown.   Chinese families find it a great place to see old friends, for almost everybody goes to **YUM CHA** on a Sunday morning.

This type of lunch can only be enjoyed in a restaurant because the little items served are so many and so varied. **(If you were to make all these tasty treats at home the pleasure of the occasion would be taken from you!)**

To my many friends in the Bay Area, you are truly fortunate. In San Francisco, there are many tea lunch shops. **YUM CHA** is served from 10:00 A.M. on through 3:00 P.M.. You may delight in trying each of the shops in order to discover your favorite. Each has its own personality, and each will usually have one item that is "better here than anywhere else in town".

As an introduction, try **ASIA GARDEN.** This is a restaurant that is fairly new, and patterned after the great tea parlors of the Orient. It has a continual atmosphere of bustle and excitement.

Another long-time favorite of mine is the **TUNG FONG.** This is a small shop, and the owner does not sacrifice quality for expediency.

The **YANK SING RESTAURANT** is the "Grand Daddy" of all the tea shops of recent vintage. It serves a good reliable line of tea lunch items of impressive variety.

Others you may like to try are the **GOLDEN DRAGON, LOUIE'S,** or **KUO WAH.**

Continued

HOW TO ORDER A TEA LUNCH

The little delights served in a tea lunch are called by the Chinese, **DEEM SUM**. **DEEM SUM** translated, means "touching your heart", which is indeed what these little morsels literally do.   At one sitting, there must be at least twenty to thirty different kinds of **DEEM SUM** that will be brought to your table! It may interest you to know that the price you will pay for your **YUM CHA**, or **DEEM SUM**, lunch will be according to the number of dishes you have chosen. Each little dish on the tray will have 2, 3, 4, or 6 pieces on it. If you have chosen one that is expensive, there will be a second little plate under the one containing the food. Some items are brought to the table in round bamboo steamers. At the end of the lunch the hostess will count the number of little dishes and bamboo steamers on your table and charge you accordingly. **(You should also be aware that there are four general classes of these items.)**

The first step in Yum Cha is the selection of your tea. The waiter will ask you for your choice, and, for the uninitiated, I would suggest **PO NAY**, which is a mild tea and very good with tea lunch. Or try **LOONG JAING (Dragon's Well), LOOK ON (Six Virtues)**, or good ol' **JASMINE!** Incidentally, when your teapot is empty and it is time for a refill, act the expert and do as the Chinese do...Merely turn the cover of your teapot upside down, or on its side. This is the universal signal that says to all tea room waiters, "My teapot is empty; how about a refill?"

Now the fun begins! No need to ask for a menu! The food will come to you! It is carried out on trays, or carted out to you by sweet little Chinese girls. Choose anything that you see to your liking, by merely nodding your head or pointing. It will be served to you. Do not be carried away with any one item! Eat sparingly of each, and try them all! Sip your tea, and visit with one another of your party. That is the magic of **YUM CHA!**

There are **four main groups of food** from which to choose. The **first group** includes the steamed dishes, such as shrimp dumplings, pork dumplings, half-moon dumplings, pork buns, and others of similar nature. The **second group** would be the **LO MEI** or variety group, containing such items as paper wrapped chicken, black bean spareribs, pickled mustard greens, duck's feet, etc. The **third group** contains the deep-fried items such as egg rolls, rice rolls, pork triangles, taro triangles, etc., while the **fourth group** includes the sweets or desserts, such as sugar gelatin cake, sponge cake, Chinese doughnuts and custard cups.

Additionally, you may order won ton soup, chow mein and chow fun **(Chinese rice noodles)** in all tea lunch restaurants.

In the larger restaurants, you will see casseroles of rice offered. These contain chicken, pork, and mushrooms. This method of cooking imparts all the flavors of the various ingredients into the rice and makes it truly an enjoyable eating experience. **(Share one of these dishes with the members of your party if you haven't discovered how delicious Chinese rice dishes can be!)**

I have introduced many of my students to this delightful pastime, as part of our Chinatown shopping trip, and they have always been extremely pleased. For those of you who are fortunate enough to live in the Bay Area, I urge you to discover the joy of **YUM CHA** for yourselves.

Note: Although I have mentioned the names of a few of the "Tea Lunch" restaurants, this information is in no way an endorsement or an advertisement for any of these establishments.

THE NAMES AND LOCATIONS OF SOME SAN FRANCISCO TEA-LUNCH RESTAURANTS

Asia Garden	772 Pacific Avenue
Golden Dragon	822 Washington Street
Kuo Wah	950 Grant Avenue
Louie's	1014 Grant Avenue
Tung Fong	808 Pacific Avenue
Yank Sing	617 Broadway Street

TEA LUNCH SPECIALTIES

Name	Chinese Name	Chinese Characters
Barbecued Pork Buns	Cha Siu Bau	义燒飽
Shrimp Dumplings	Har Gow	蝦餃
Pork Dumplings	Gee Yuk Shiu Mai	豬肉燒賣
Half Moon Dumplings	Fun Gor	粉果
Paper Wrapped Chicken	Gee-Bow Gai	紙包雞
Black Bean Spareribs, Steamed	See Jup Pai Gwut	蒸排骨
Pickled Mustard Greens	Shuen Guy Choy	酸菜
Duck's Feet	Op Gurk	鹵水鴨脚
Egg Rolls	Choon Guen	春卷

Continued

Tea Lunch Specialties (Continued)

Name	Chinese Name	Chinese Characters
Rice Rolls	Gnaw Mai Guen	糯米卷
Pork Triangles	Jeu Yuk Gok	咸水角
Taro Triangles	Oo Gok	芋角
Sugar Gelatin Cake	Bok Tong Go	白糖糕
Custard Cups	Don Tot	蛋撻
Chinese Doughnuts	Jeen Dui	煎堆

FOOD STUFFS USED IN CHINESE COOKING

Name	Chinese Name	Chinese Characters
BAMBOO SHOOTS	JOOK SUN	竹筍
BEAN CAKE	FOO YUEH	腐乳
BEAN SAUCE	MIN SEE JERNG	元豉醬
BEAN SPROUTS	NGAH CHOY	牙菜
BEAN THREADS	FUN SEE	粉絲
BLACK BEANS, SALTED	DOW SEE	豆豉
BLACK MUSHROOMS	DOONG GOO	冬姑
BOK CHOY	BOK CHOY	白菜
CANDIED WINTER MELON	TONG GWAH	糖瓜

Continued

Food Stuffs Used In Chinese Cooking (Continued)

Name	Chinese Name	Chinese Characters
CHILI PASTE WITH GARLIC	LAHT JIU JERNG	辣椒醬
CHINESE BLACK VINEGAR	TIM CHEU	甜醋
CHINESE MUSTARD GREENS	GUY CHOY	芥菜
CHINESE RADISH	CHOY PO	菜脯
CHINESE ROCK SUGAR	BING TONG	冰糖
CHINESE SAUSAGE	LOP CHERNG	臘腸
CLOUD FUNGUS	WUN NGEE	雲耳
DEEP-FRIED NOODLES	YEE MEIN	伊麵
DRIED BEAN CURD	FOO JOOK	腐竹

Continued

Food Stuffs Used In Chinese Cooking (Continued)

Name	Chinese Name	Chinese Characters
DRIED OCTOPUS	BAHT JOW YEU	八爪魚
DRIED ORANGE PEEL, CHINESE	GWOH PEI	菓皮
DRIED SHRIMP	HA MAI	蝦米
EGG ROLL SKINS	CHOON GUEN PEI	春卷皮
FIVE SPICE POWDER	HERNG LIU FUN	五香粉
FRESH NOODLES	MEIN	麵
GLUTINOUS RICE POWDER	GNAW MAI FUN	糯米粉
HOISIN SAUCE	HOISIN JERNG	海鮮醬
LILY FLOWER (GOLDEN NEEDLE)	GUM JUM	金針

Continued

Food Stuffs Used In Chinese Cooking (Continued)

Name	Chinese Name	Chinese Characters
LOTUS ROOT	LIN NGAU	蓮藕
MINI SWEET CORN	YUK MAI SUN	玉米筍
MUSTARD POWDER	GAI LAHT	芥辣
NAPA CABBAGE	SIU CHOY	紹菜
OYSTER SAUCE	HO YAU	蠔油
PEPPERCORN, SZCHUAN TYPE	FAH JIU	花椒
PICKLED MUSTARD	JAH CHOY	炸菜
RED DATES	HEUNG JO	紅棗
RICE STICKS	PY MEI FUN	排米粉

Continued

Food Stuffs Used In Chinese Cooking (Continued)

Name	Chinese Name	Chinese Characters
ROASTING SALT	SIU YIM	燒鹽
ROUND DUMPLING SKINS	SHIU MAI PEI	燒賣皮
SESAME OIL	GEE MAH YAU	芝麻油
SESAME SEEDS	GEE MAH	芝麻
SNOW PEAS	HAW LON DOW	荷蘭豆
SOY SAUCE, DARK	LO CHEOW	老抽
SOY SAUCE, THIN	SANG CHEOW	生抽
STAR ANISE	BAKT GOK	八角
SWEET AND SOUR GINGER	TIM SHEUN GERNG	甜酸羌

Continued

Food Stuffs Used In Chinese Cooking (Continued)

Name	Chinese Name	Chinese Characters
SWEET RICE	GNAW MAI	糯米
WATER CHESTNUTS	MAH TAI	馬蹄
WATER CHESTNUT POWDER	MAH TAI FUN	馬蹄粉
WINTER MELON	DOONG GWAH	冬瓜
WON TON SKINS	WON.TON PEI	雲吞皮
WOOD FUNGUS	MOOK NGEE	木耳

CHINESE BANQUET INFORMATION

Now that you have come to the end of the book, and you have had a chance to try my recipes, it is time for you to put all of your skill to work in preparing a typical Chinese banquet for your friends.

In a restaurant a Chinese banquet is usually served to ten people, seated around a circular dining table to facilitate conversation, conviviality, and dining. The banquet is usually composed of eight dishes, and the dishes are chosen to compliment each other as to taste, aroma, texture and appearance.

Try to serve each dish to your guests with just the proper interval of time spaced in between, so that they may enjoy each dish in its turn, have ample time to converse with their neighbors, and look expectantly to the next masterpiece.

Most chopping and cutting may be done the night before and the food kept in plastic bags or plastic boxes in the refrigerator.

In planning ahead and organizing, give thought to the utensils that you will require, as well as the food preparation. All preparation can go for nought, if all of a sudden you find that there is no tureen in which to put the soup!

One more tip...Candle or electric warmers are very helpful in keeping the prepared dishes warm. **(It is not wise to put them in a heated oven as this tends to dry out most foods.)** Using a warmer allows you time to relax and enjoy your company!

SUGGESTED CHINESE BANQUET MENUS

MENU I

Won Ton Soup

Cashew Nut Chicken

Pork Spareribs With Black Bean Sauce

Bean Sprouts With Mixed Vegetables

Steamed Rice

Almond Milk Curd

PREPARATION ORDER SO AS TO ELIMINATE SOME LAST MINUTE WORK

1. **ALMOND MILK CURD** may be made 2 days in advance.
2. Cashew nuts may be deep-fried 2 days in advance.
3. Cut all meats and vegetables the night before the banquet.
4. Prepare **PORK SPARERIBS** approx. 4 hrs. in advance. **(Reheat for 5 min. before serving time.)**
5. Wrap **WON TON** a few hrs. beforehand. Cover with saran wrap or foil, and keep refrigerated or at room temperature. **(Cook just before serving time.)**
6. Prepare won ton broth a few hrs. in advance. Bring it to a boil before serving.
7. **CASHEW NUT CHICKEN** may be prepared several hours earlier, with the exception of steps **9 and 13**, which need to be prepared at the last minute.
8. Rice may be cooked approx. an hour in advance if you have a Japanese rice cooker with a "warm" setting. Otherwise, cook the rice according to the **STEAMED RICE** recipe and reheat by steaming for about 8 min. just before serving.
9. **BEAN SPROUTS WITH MIXED VEGETABLES** must be cooked at the last minute, otherwise they will lose their crispness.

MENU II

Chicken Salad

Sweet & Sour Pork

Spiced Cabbage

Fried Rice

Oyster Beef

Fortune Cookies (purchased)

PREPARATION ORDER SO AS TO ELIMINATE SOME LAST MINUTE WORK

1. Make **SWEET AND SOUR SAUCE** 1 - 2 weeks in advance. Keep refrigerated.

2. Two days in advance deep-fry the rice sticks and peanuts; also toast the sesame seeds for the **CHICKEN SALAD.** Keep them in a closed container.

3. Cut all meats and vegetables the night before the banquet.

4. Prepare the **SPICED CABBAGE** up to 8 hrs. in advance and refrigerate.

5. **CHICKEN SALAD** can be prepared approx. 5 hrs. earlier with the exception of step 12, which should be done just before serving time. Store salad at room temperature.

6. Prepare **FRIED RICE** approx. 4 hrs. in advance, omitting the shredded lettuce. Reheat by stir-frying for 3 min. Add the shredded lettuce at that time.

7. The **SWEET AND SOUR PORK** may be prepared approx. 3 hours in advance, with the exception of steps 8, 10 and 11, which must be done just before serving time.

8. **OYSTER BEEF** must be prepared at the last minute.

MENU III

Sizzling Rice Soup

Egg Rolls

Paper Wrapped Chicken

Tomato Beef

Steamed Rice

Steamed Egg Custard

PREPARATION ORDER SO AS TO ELIMINATE SOME LAST MINUTE WORK

1. Cook and bake rice for **SIZZLING RICE SOUP** approx. 2 days in advance. Put in a tightly closed container for future use.

2. Cut all meats and vegetables the night before the banquet.

3. Prepare and deep-fry the **EGG ROLLS** and **PAPER WRAPPED CHICKEN** from 3 - 5 hrs. in advance Put them in a roaster and cover with foil in preparation for reheating later. Reheat in 325 degree oven for 12 - 15 min. just before serving time.

4. Steam the **EGG CUSTARD** approx. 2 hrs. in advance. Keep refrigerated. **(If you prefer to serve the custard hot, it has to be prepared at the last minute.)**

5. **TOMATO BEEF** can be prepared approx. 2 hrs. earlier, with the exception of steps 9 and 10, which need to be done at the last minute.

6. Rice may be cooked approx. an hour in advance if you have a Japanese rice cooker with a "warm" setting. Otherwise, cook the rice according to the **STEAMED RICE** recipe and reheat by steaming for about 8 minutes.

7. Prepare soup stock for **SIZZLING RICE SOUP** an hour in advance.

8. Prepare the deep-fried rice and bring the soup stock to a boil so that they are both ready at the same time, which will be just prior to serving.

MENU IV

Spiced Shrimp

Chicken Chow Mein

Curried Chicken With Potatoes

Stir-Fried Bok Choy

Steamed Rice

Mandarin Glazed Apple and Banana

PREPARATION ORDER SO AS TO ELIMINATE SOME LAST MINUTE WORK

1. Pan-fry noodles for chow mein either 2 days in advance and refrigerate, or pan-fry the night before and keep at room temperature.

2. Cut all meats and vegetables the night before the banquet. Be sure to soak the potatoes in cold water so as to prevent discoloration.

3. Make **CHICKEN CHOW MEIN** approx. 4 hrs in advance. Reheat in 350 degree oven for 10 - 14 min. before serving time.

4. Prepare **CURRIED CHICKEN WITH POTATOES** approx. 3 hrs. earlier. Reheat for 5 min. before serving time.

5. Up to step 5, the **SPICED SHRIMP** may be prepared approx. 2 hrs. in advance. Steps 5 - 7 must be done just before serving time.

6. Rice may be cooked an hour in advance if you have a Japanese rice cooker with a "warm" setting. Otherwise, cook the rice according to the **STEAMED RICE** recipe and reheat by steaming for about 8 minutes just before serving.

7. **STIR-FRIED BOK CHOY** must be prepared at the last minute.

8. While the guests are relaxing, prepare the **MANDARIN GLAZED APPLE AND BANANA**. This must be done at serving time.

178

INDEX

A   **Page**

Abalone
   in Oyster Sauce   99
   in Bok Choy   100
Almond Milk Curd   147

B

Bamboo Shoots   16
   With Chinese Mushrooms   115
Barbecued Pork
   Buns   148
   Chinese   86
Bean Cake   16
   Chow Bean Cake   117
   Stuffed Bean Cake   126
Bean Curd, Dried   19
Bean Sauce   16
   With Chicken   51
Bean Sprouts   16
   With Mixed Vegetables   113
Beef
   in Hoisin Sauce   79
   in Oyster Sauce   80
   Ground Beef & Napa Cabbage   84
   Stew, Cantonese   81
   With Fuzzy Squash   82
   With Tomato   85
Bird's Nest Soup   36
Black Beans, Salted   16
   With Spareribs   91

B (Continued)   **Page**

Black Mushrooms   17
Boiled Chicken   52
Bok Choy   17
   Stir-Fried   125
   With Abalone   100
Broccoli With Chicken   114
Buns, Barbecued Pork   148

C

Cabbage
   Spiced   122
   With Chicken   58
Cashew Nut
   Prawns   101
   Chicken   54
Chicken
   Bean Sauce   51
   Boiled   52
   Cashew Nut   54
   Crispy   62
   Curried With Potato   63
   Fried   66
   Gizzards   68
   Meatball Soup   37
   Paper Wrapped   69
   Pineapple   71
   Salad   59
   Steamed   73
   Stock   18

C (Continued)	Page		D	Page
Chicken			Deep-Frying	11
Topping on Noodles	131		Dried Bean Curd	19
Whisky Soup	38		Duck and Potatoes	64
Wings in Soy Sauce	72		Dumplings, Steamed Pork	161
With Asparagus	56			
With Asparagus (Cold)	61			
With Bean Cake Sauce	57		E	
With Broccoli	114			
With Cabbage	58		Egg	
Chinese			Custard, Steamed	78
Barbecued Pork	86		Flower Soup	39
Doughnuts	27		Foo Yung	74
Fried Dumplings	30		Steamed	77
Mushrooms With Bamboo Shoots	115		With Green Peas & Shrimp	76
Sausage	18		Eggplant, Spiced	123
String Beans With Prawns	116		Egg Roll	31
Chopsticks	3		Skins	19
Techniques in Using	5		Wrapping	32
Chow Mein				
Beef	128			
Chicken	130		F	
Tomato Beef	136			
Cleaver	6		Five Spice Powder	19
Cloud Fungus	18		Flavored Salt	59
Coconut & Preserved Sweet and			Fried Rice	138
Sour Ginger	151			
Cold Chicken With Asparagus	61			
Cornstarch, Use of	18		G	
Crab, Stir-Fried	109			
Curried Tripe	83		Ginger Root	19
Cutting Techniques	13		Gizzards, Chicken	68

G (Continued)	Page
Glutinous Rice Powder	19
Golden Needle (Lily Flower)	20

H

Ham With Bean Threads	87
Hoisin Sauce	19
With Spareribs	88
Hot and Sour Soup	40
Hot Pepper Toss	118
Hot Spiced Oil	152

L

Lettuce Soup	42
Lily Flower (Golden Needle)	20
Lotus Root	20
Soup	43
With Pork	119

M

Mandarin Glazed Apple & Banana	153
Mongolian Fire Pot	154
Mushrooms	
in Oyster Sauce	120
With Bamboo Shoots	115
Mustard Powder	20

N	Page
Napa Cabbage	21
New Year's Cake	156
Noodles	
Deep-Fried	21
Fresh	21
in Gravy	133
in Oyster Sauce	134
Soup	35
Spiced	135
With Chicken Topping	131
Northern Vegetables Covered	
With Egg	121

O

Oil	21
Hot Spiced	152
Oyster Sauce	21

P

Pan-Frying	12
Pickled	
Carrots & Daikon Radish	157
Mustard Greens	158
Pigs Feet in Vinegar Sauce	89
Pork	
Chinese Barbecued	86

P (Continued)   **Page**

Pork
Chinese Sausage Cakes, Steamed	90
Spareribs With Black Beans	91
Sweet and Sour	96
Twice Cooked	98
With Chinese Radish, Steamed	95
With Lotus Root	119
With Pickled Mustard	93
With String Beans	94
Pot Stickers	159

Prawns (Shrimp)
Cashew Nut	101
Curried	102
Pan-Fried	103
Shelling & Deveining	104
Spiced	105
With Black Bean Sauce, Steamed	106
With Chinese String Beans	116

R

Red Dates	22
Rice	22
Fried	138
Soup	44
Steamed	139
Sweet	140
Rice Sticks	22

S   **Page**

Salmon, Cantonese	107
Salt, Flavored	59
Sand Dab	108
Seaweed Soup	47
Sesame Oil	22

Shrimp (Prawns)
Balls	33
Toast	34
Sizzling Rice Soup	48
Snow Peas	23
Soy Sauce	23

Spareribs
in Hoisin Sauce	88
in Black Bean Sauce	91

Spiced
Cabbage	122
Oil	152
Shrimp (Prawns)	105
Spinach With Bean Cake Paste	124
Squab, Fried	67
Squid With Snow Peas	111
Star Anise	23

Steamed
Chicken	73
Chinese Pork Sausage Cakes	90
Egg	77
Egg Custard	78
Pork Dumplings	161
Pork With Chinese Radish	95

S (Continued)	Page
Steamed	
Prawns With Black Bean Sauce	106
Rice	139
Salmon, Cantonese	107
Sand Dab	108
Steaming	10
Stewing	12
Stir-Frying	9
Sweet and Sour Pork	96
T	
Table of Measures	26
Tea	24
Tomato Beef	85
Tripe, Curried	83
Twice Cooked Pork	98

W	Page
Watercress Soup	49
Water Chestnuts	25
Wine	25
Winter Melon	25
Soup	50
Wok	8
Mei	1
Won Ton	
Basic	141
Deep-Fried	143
in Gravy	144
in Oyster Sauce	145
Skins	25
Soup	146
Wrapping	142
Wood Fungus	26

ORDER FORM

To order extra copies of **CHOPSTICKS, CLEAVER AND WOK** cut out order form below and send with check or money order for $4.50 per copy. California residents add 6% sales tax, or 6½% if you live in a BART District county.

Jennie Low
P. O. Box 759
El Cerrito, Ca. 94530

We pay postage for delivery within the continental U.S.

- -

To:
Jennie Low
P. O. Box 759
El Cerrito, Ca. 94530

Please send me _____ copies of **CHOPSTICKS, CLEAVER AND WOK**.

I enclose $ _____ .   ☐ Check   ☐ Money Order

(PLEASE PRINT)

NAME _____

ADDRESS _____

CITY _____ STATE _____ ZIP _____